The Place of the Parish

MARTIN ROBINSON

The Place of the Parish

scm press

© Martin Robinson 2020

Published in 2020 by SCM Press
Editorial office
3rd Floor, Invicta House,
108–114 Golden Lane,
London EC1Y 0TG, UK
www.scmpress.co.uk

SCM Press is an imprint of Hymns Ancient & Modern Ltd
(a registered charity)

Hymns Ancient & Modern® is a registered trademark of
Hymns Ancient & Modern Ltd
13a Hellesdon Park Road, Norwich,
Norfolk NR6 5DR, UK

British Library Cataloguing in Publication data

A catalogue record for this book is available
from the British Library

978 0 334 05825 0

Printed and bound by
CPI Group (UK) Ltd

Contents

Introduction

The growing popularity of pilgrimages of various kinds draws attention to the significance of particular places. Many authors notice that certain of these are referred to as 'holy' places, and speculate as to what it might be that marks them out as pointing to a reality beyond themselves. But whether a place is regarded as holy or simply meaningful, in terms of the lived reality of those who were born and brought up there, we can be aware that where we live and spend our time creates a narrative that helps to shape and interpret our lives. To some extent, we see ourselves through the lens of the stories and experiences that connect us to a physical context.

Behind this book lies a number of convictions and working assumptions. Together with many colleagues, I have been working for several decades on key questions about faith, the church and mission. It has become increasingly clear that the Church in the West is undergoing a creative and often painful re-imagination of its identity, purpose and relationship with the mission field in which it is set. We can increasingly see that the future of the Church is not about programmes, techniques and methods, but is about leadership, about how we discern what God is doing; and both of these things hinge on how we interpret the context in which we are located. The place to which we are called is more than just an evangelistic opportunity. Just as God came to us in the incarnation, so the Church must take seriously our presence in our locale.

That commitment to the local, to the parish, also contains a conviction that we can begin to grasp what God is up to through local narratives. In Acts 16 we read Luke's account of a process of discernment and call. The Holy Spirit prevented Paul and his followers acting in some localities and directed them to others. The Church was grounded in a place of prayer among a group of women meeting by a river. This narrative conveys a great deal about the faith we hold and the God in whom we believe. In the same way, the stories we tell about encounters between our God and people in local settings are deeply significant in terms of the re-imagining of what God is seeking to do with his church in these times of challenge and change.

Together with partners in North America, a number of us in the UK have sought to capture some of these stories and to tell them in both video format and in written text in an online format, the *Journal of Missional Practice*. Some of the thinking in this book is a reflection of the work of the journal and also of material that is contained in an MA in Missional Leadership offered by ForMission College, which I also lead.

I am particularly indebted to my colleague Mary Publicover, who works closely with me on the journal and who has also helped to shape elements of the MA in Missional Leadership. Much of the text in Chapter 1 has come from work contributed by Mary to one of the modules in the MA that works with the theme of place. Mary and I work with the stories that appear in the journal. These stories have helped to shape my reflection on place and its importance.

When I began writing this book I had in mind the total landscape of the western world, partly because I am interested in the West as a unique mission field, and partly because I have lived in the USA for a period of time, and travel widely in North America, Europe and Australia. However, as the book developed, I became increasingly aware that it is very difficult, if not impossible, to do justice to the difference between these various contexts. Therefore, the book has centred on the context of England with an awareness of these other contexts in the background.

I am also aware that the 'parish' is a difficult word because different denominations respond to the term in a wide variety of ways. Because 'parish' can also have a particular meaning in terms of local government – a parish council – I have not tried to create a single interpretation of the term. Context partly produces its own definition and to a certain extent I rely on the reader to interpret the meaning of parish in relation to their own experience and context.

1

Why is Place Important?

The geneticist Steve Jones makes the arresting claim that the invention of the bicycle was a huge factor in promoting the development of a healthy human gene pool. The point he is making is simply that before the invention of the bicycle we tended to marry people who lived within walking distance of where we lived. Especially in rural areas, that limited the gene pool to a relatively small number of people.

Following the invention of the bicycle, the availability of the car further extended the range of people we might be likely to marry. Following that, the tendency of large percentages of the population to attend university meant that many people might marry others who had previously lived anywhere in the country. Still further, the development of significant patterns of international migration and globalization in terms of employment and trade means that our children and grandchildren might well marry partners from other continents and not just other parts of our own nation. So the bicycle, Steve Jones argues, helped to set off a mixing of the gene pool that on the whole has improved the overall health of the human race.

Leaving aside the issue of genetic diversity, the reality of mobility is evident from our own experience of life. I often ask the question when visiting local congregations, 'How many people grew up in this neighbourhood?' and 'How many people came into this congregation because their parents were members of this church?' The results vary somewhat depending on whether the congregation is located in a city, a market town or a rural area. But no matter what the location, it is always a minority of people who grew up in that area. Most churches are populated by people who have moved from another location.[1]

Steve Jones's description of the development of our tendency towards mobility in the modern world carries with it the suggestion that increased mobility has made the local become less significant. In many communities, local shops, local schools, hospitals, pubs, post offices and banks have been closing. Even in larger and more prosperous towns and cities, suburban shopping streets have seen familiar shops closing, partly under pressure from larger supermarkets, out-of-town shopping centres and shopping on the internet. The car, far more than the bicycle, has been a factor in denuding local communities of the rich variety available within walking distance. The shops with which we were so familiar have been replaced by charity shops, betting shops, and fast food outlets.

New housing estates, especially those built by developers who have a commuter customer in mind, are increasingly designed with no amenities such as shops, schools, community centres or churches. Places where it is possible to meet, to interact with other people, to engage in meaningful conversation, are simply not available in increasing numbers of neighbourhoods. The term 'dormitory community' has been coined to describe developments where people only live to eat and sleep. Their remaining time is taken up with very long hours at work combined with commuting.

Gated communities and secure apartment blocks, which can only be accessed by the residents of those homes, make it increasingly difficult to meet and greet even those who might live in the same street or adjoining properties. Our towns and cities have become simultaneously crowded and lonely places in which to live.

The erosion of our sense of local community is reflected to some extent in patterns of church attendance. Large regional churches, whether located in city centres or suburban areas, attract congregations from many local communities. With increased mobility, parish boundaries have become irrelevant. What matters is locating a church that features worship styles and programmes that are welcoming and attractive. Sometimes the worship areas look and feel more like vast warehouses where windows are unimportant, as is the immediate neighbourhood.

There are those who argue that none of this matters, that forms of community are changing and new kinds of community are emerging. Particularly in larger capital cities where there is a good public transport infrastructure, where a person lives is not as important as the networks of people with whom it's possible to build strong relationships. Some larger churches in London base their small groups in coffee bars located near tube stations. Others suggest that the internet provides meaningful connection and community for those who might be described as forming 'affinity' groups. Two recent authors explain the paradigm shift in such thinking between geography as a location for belonging and affinity based elsewhere, with the following illustration:

> Recently, Andrew's father was trying to understand how the local twenty over competition is structured and players are selected. He had followed cricket for his whole life with one structure and suddenly there were new and unusual competitions and players. For his generation, cricket is now a somewhat incomprehensible activity. So, he asked his twelve-year-old grandchildren to explain. For young students of the game, fluidity is all they know. One of the sticking points that Andrew's father pressed them on was what region, state or country the teams were representing. For someone of his generation, cricket was not just entertainment but also about representation. He couldn't understand the point of meaningless entertainment in a private competition when it came to cricket. His grandchildren had a completely different perspective and struggled to understand the nature of his

question. Both generations needed to make a paradigm shift to understand the other's world.[2]

However, it may be that this is not an either-or situation. It is possible that affinity groups, or non-geographic ways of connecting, might add another layer alongside ways of belonging that are more connected to place. It's fine for those who do not yet have the commitments of marriage and children to travel across cities to form community but arguably that does not work as people form other attachments – and possibly even move out of cities in order to create a different, more local, lifestyle.

There is an argument to suggest that cyber communities are really pseudo communities where the real self is not revealed. They are not so much about intimacy and vulnerability as entertainment and exploration. Such communities are invaluable for the sharing of knowledge or information, for maintaining relationships that have been founded elsewhere, but there are limits to the kind of relationship that can be maintained in cyberspace. Those who meet online eventually meet in person in order to test whether a compatible relationship can be formed, whatever the promise of online communication might suggest. There is an inescapable reality that we are not just minds or souls. We are embodied beings and that physical fact creates both joy and limitations. There is an important sense in which to be human is to be placed.[3] If you have a body, then you must be connected to a place or places.

A community too is a placed reality. The sense of place is created through nature and through human creativity. The streets, shops, parks, memories and local stories may have been collecting for many generations. A church community will take its own place within that setting. If a church wishes to respond to God's presence and work in that community, day by day, and through the generations, it must learn how to be present among the houses, streets and stories.

John Inge argues that through our Greek intellectual heritage, powerful now in modernity and postmodernity, this fundamental part of being human has been neglected.[4] Greek thought, particularly associated with Plato and Neoplatonism, tended to prefer abstraction and generalization rather than the immediate, particular reality. The idea of a tree and the idea of a house were considered to be more significant than this actual, specific tree or house. Susceptible to the bias of the times, Christians have tended to spiritualize talk of place in the Bible, forgetting that we have been created as embodied and placed.

Andrew Rumsey quotes John Inge as suggesting that a Christian understanding of place has a sacramental quality. He notes that Inge suggests that place is the seat of relations between God and the world.[5] Rumsey also draws on the thought of Doreen Massey, who says that space or place is socially constructed but society is also spatially constructed.[6] In other words, it is impossible to have a social structure that is entirely abstract; there needs to be a physical location. Equally, places draw much of their significance from a complex interaction with people – their beliefs, their stories, their history, their lives.

There is a need to recover this aspect of our personhood, and to look again at Scripture and theology in relation to place. It is important to grapple with Scripture to understand the significance of this phenomenon in order to consider how to read our own community.

Place in the Old Testament

According to Walter Brueggemann, place is the setting for connection and commitment. There is a continuing temptation to a disconnected freedom, space, which is strongly represented in postmodernity. In his view, our nature as embodied beings – and therefore placed beings – needs to be acknowledged:

Place is space which has historical meanings, where some

things have happened which are now remembered and which provide continuity and identity across generations. Place is space in which important words have been spoken which have established identity, defined vocation and envisioned destiny. Place is space in which vows have been exchanged, promises have been made, and demands have been issued. Place is indeed a protest against the unpromising pursuit of space. It is a declaration that our humanness cannot be found in escape, detachment, absence of commitments and undefined freedom.[7]

Looking at the Old Testament narratives, Brueggemann describes land as an essential third component in the relationship between Israel and Yahweh. He sees that it is land that makes that relationship possible, although there are many twists and turns in that unfolding three-way relationship. Yahweh and his people experience one another through their shared place. Some of that sharing includes the loss of place, or sojourning, as Abram leaves his country, his kindred and his father's house, responding to a promise.[8] Some of the sharing involves wandering in the desert, when the memory of the promise of land was weak. Some of that sharing includes exile, as Israel, having lost its relationship with Yahweh, loses the land too. In exile the sharing comes to mean again the promise of land, the hope of land and a longing for home.

He sees the core idea in Israel's relationship with Yahweh and land as being one of grasp and gift. When Israel responds to the promise of the gift, and receives the gift of land with gratitude, caring for the land and its people, then this three-way relationship thrives. When Israel's elite is tempted to manage this gift, and to grasp it, and to exclude and enslave the poor, then eventually the land is lost. The Lord, people and place are inextricably woven together in harmony.[9]

Walter Brueggemann describes his discovery of this central theme almost as a conversion. He had, with other theologians of the twentieth century, tended towards a hermeneutic of time and pivotal events: 'the mighty deeds of God in history'.[10] But he explains that the twentieth-century failure of the promise of the cities alerted him and others to the human need for a place and a home.[11] Scripture speaks of community and home, rather than individuality and the search for meaning.

Brueggemann was also aware that acknowledging the significance of land in itself makes quite a fundamental shift in how we may view our shared lives with God. It draws the focus back to God, who sustains us in our communities in our ordinary lives, rather than in the occasional miraculous intervention.

Place in the New Testament

The focus on the land of Israel and on Jerusalem shifts in the New Testament and becomes centred on Jesus rather than on a temple or city. However, through the incarnation, the body, and therefore a particular time and a particular place, become raised in their significance:

> We might say, therefore, that it is clear from the incarnation that places are the seat of relations or the place of meeting and activity in the interaction between God and the world, and argue further that place is therefore a fundamental category of human and spiritual experience.[12]

Jesus looks ahead to his Father's house, to the place he has promised to prepare for us. Tom Wright argues firmly against the Platonism of the Christian tradition, and for a New Heaven and a New Earth that renews, rather than abolishes Earth:

> The New Testament never imagines that, when the new heavens and new earth arrive, God will say in effect, 'well, that first creation wasn't so good after all, was it? Aren't you glad we've got rid of all that space, time and matter?' Rather,

we must envisage a world in which the present creation, which we think of in those three dimensions, is enhanced, taken up into God's larger purposes no doubt, but certainly not abandoned.[13]

Place in modernity

According to John Inge, place was becoming eclipsed as a concept even in the roots of the Western intellectual tradition. He describes this as a tension between place and space. We experience place, it is a primary part of the experience of being human, and we experience it as particular places, which impact us. Space, however, is an inert void, which extends for ever, into infinity. It is broken down into specific places but these may be of reduced significance. Certainly in the view of John Inge, Greek Neoplatonism influenced intellectual thought towards space.

This trend was exacerbated in modernity, first through the advent of scientific method, which wanted to be able to simplify and generalize. 'Place makes a poor abstraction', complains the anthropologist Clifford Geertz.[14] Particular places, with their own history, and unique characteristics, resist modernity's tendency to generalize and categorize. Place is experienced in very subjective ways. Modernity, as epitomized through science, drives towards objectivity.

Second, as modernity began to understand the universe as driven through time by the relationship of cause and effect, a preference for time over place grew in academia. These are difficult ideas to grasp and communicate. We are helped by the reflections of the philosopher Edward S. Casey, who comments on the power of modernity's disregard for place in this way:

In the past three centuries in the West – the period of modernity – place has come to be not only neglected but actively suppressed. Owing to the triumph of the natural and social sciences in this same period, any serious talk of place has been regarded as regressive or trivial. A discourse has emerged whose exclusive cosmological foci are Time and Space. When the two were combined by twentieth-century physicists into the amalgam 'space-time' the overlooking of place was only continued by other means. For an entire epoch, place has been regarded as an impoverished second cousin of Time and Space, those two colossal cosmic partners towering over modernity.[15]

These developments in scientific thought have been accompanied by advances in technology that have also tended to reduce the significance of place, at least for the powerful. When I first began to travel internationally, the differences between shops in the high street and prices in the high street were very noticeable from nation to nation, including the goods on offer at airports themselves. Today there is an almost shocking similarity in the appearance of high streets across the world. The same international brands have become powerfully present in every city and nation. Economic globalization erodes the differences in places, as the same commercial powers appear in every town: McDonald's, Barclays, Coca-Cola, Toyota, Canon, to name a few. As reflections of the growing influence of the powerful, these developments are not necessarily benign. Globalization has arguably had a profound impact on the poor by breaking the support structures that a grounding in the local tends to produce.

Rediscovering place

Heidegger gave voice to a distress that he claimed flows from this experience of placelessness. According to John Inge, he saw this as an outcome of modernity's tendency to impose a gap between subject and object.[16] We have learnt to see ourselves as separate from, yet acting on, the things that surround us. But for

Heidegger that separation is an illusion, as we are vulnerable, connected and sustained by our physical context. He uses the expression 'immersion' to better describe how we relate to the place where we may be. He also uses the German word *Dasein* for human being, literally a 'being-there'.

Michel de Certeau, the social theorist, has written about modernity experienced in the oppression of a city.[17] Writing in a poetic and evocative manner he proposes that concepts of time or progress are dominant, and that space itself is overlooked. So when he observes New York from the top of the World Trade Center he describes it as laid out like a map, systematized and conceptualized. Part of this conceptualization is about the power and control exercised within it and through it: 'On this concrete, steel and glass stage, bounded by the cold water of two oceans (the Atlantic and the American) the tallest letters in the world create this gigantesque rhetoric of excess in expenditure and production.'[18] De Certeau writes of city streets and systems and the 'places where you can no longer believe in anything'. He describes a process where named places with their own stories are removed and replaced by numbers, and 'the habitable city is wiped out'.[19] He writes of a flat, mapped, known and numbered world without stories, without wonder and without mystery.

However, at ground level people are moving about through this city, inscribing their own practices among the remaining names and the memories of stories: 'It is through the opportunity they afford of storing up pregnant silences and inarticulate stories – or rather through their ability to create cellars and attics everywhere – that local legends create exits, ways of leaving and re-entering, and thus habitable spaces.'[20] For de Certeau, it is the very ordinary acts of walking to work and eating meals that create social space. These activities become the simple ways in which we all, as embodied people, connect – physically, viscerally – with our immediate environment. The advent of postmodernity has released a renewed appreciation of the particular. Modernity deals in absolutes, generalizations, universals or abstractions. But postmodern theorists like de Certeau have challenged grand narratives of modern efficiency and power. Postmodernity has provided the opportunity for a renewed appreciation of particular places with their particular stories.

Storied place

Geographers, recovering from modernity's disregard for place, now note a relational view of place, which through its communities and history acquire an identity.[21] Places hold memories and communicate stories. Witness the significance given to the exact place of death in the roadside memorials that have appeared in recent years. A place may become what is, in effect, a very richly layered 'text' as new layers of meaning, new stories and memories are added by communities, possibly over generations. These physical symbols are powerful mediators of culture, especially when sustained by storytelling and traditions. An aspect of a place may be lost when there is no longer a community to tell its story in this way.

Because human beings are embodied and immersed in the place where they are, the stories embedded in the features of a place may powerfully impact the way people think, live and relate. These features may be man-made or natural. They may enter consciously into the imagination of a community. Or this process may be unconscious, but communicate values powerfully.

Clemens Sedmak gives an account of the story of a local legend that lingered in the imagination of the people. It became connected with local folk religion and was eventually confronted and challenged by the Roman Catholic Church in that place.[22]

Implicit stories or messages may be even more powerful. In Bournville, the home of Cadbury's chocolate factory, houses, shops, lamp posts, street signs and fences have a rural, traditional

English style. A maypole country dance lies at the centre of the village festival. This development did not occur by accident but by the very deliberate annexation by George Cadbury of inspiration gathered from the Arts and Crafts movement pioneered by individuals such as John Ruskin. Indeed, Cadbury built an art college called Ruskin Hall that stands at the very centre of Bournville, on one side of the village green, taking a place of importance alongside shops, schools, a bank, a further education college and churches. The factory that provided the wealth to create this unique experiment stands symbolically, and physically, behind the village green.

This was all part of Cadbury's desire to create a meaningful community and not just a place for his workforce to live. He also recognized that his attempts to create community required structures to support community, but ultimately stories which only those who lived in that location could create, maintain and develop. The Cadbury story, especially as the immediate family become detached from the commercial enterprise that carries their name, requires continuing generations to recover the Cadbury story, to celebrate it and to give it new layers of meaning and interpretation through contemporary events based in living communities of those who have a deep connection with that neighbourhood. It is interesting to note that in an age of increased mobility, many choose to return to Bournville in their later years because it provides a sense of belonging and of home. It is often, though not exclusively, the churches that help to develop the Cadbury story.

In contrast to the deeply rooted community experience of Bournville, T. J. Gorringe cites pseudo-communities which strive, oppressively, to maintain a façade of community life.[23] Extravagant shopping malls are often cited as representations of the 'cathedral' of consumerism. They not only express this value, they reinforce it in the culture. Elaborately tended private gardens and neglected parks may express and reinforce individualism in a place. A well or a spring may have attracted stories over time, which engage the interest of the local 'new age' communities.

The story of a place, whether it is a town, church or hill, matters because, according to the philosopher Paul Ricoeur, stories are essential to human identity. He builds on the work of the philosophers Heidegger and Gadamer, who suggest that we are *condemned to meaning*, and have a sense of ourselves as within a story that we are continuously rewriting through time.[24] As individual beings, we do not live in isolation. We are not born without connections of some kind. According to Gadamer, we are *historical beings*,[25] sustained by a tradition.

Stories can draw us into a new way of thinking about our lives. As we connect with a new story, carrying all the assumptions of tradition and history with us, we are *seized by meaning*. To use Gadamer's expression, our horizons fuse with those of the text. A new world – or new imagination – is possible, and this can occur as a new story is encountered, or as an old story is retold. This is powerful at the level of individual transformation. When the story is shared by a group, or even within a place, there may be a major impact, both positively and negatively.

So a storied place, a place that carries a powerful story, can have a great impact for good or harm. However, quoting David Harvey, T. J. Gorringe reminds us that the nature of these stories is an unfolding outcome of human creativity, and power struggles in a place.[26] The power of narrative may be used and abused.

According to John Inge, as their communities acquire memories, most places acquire a personality that is sustained by the physicality of the place, and the continuity of a remembering community. He describes the reflections of secular philosophers and geographers here:

The philosopher Edward Casey refers to time and history being so deeply inscribed in places as to be inseparable from them, and the social theorist E. V. Walker writes that place has no feelings apart from human experience there, but a place is: 'a location of experience. It evokes and organises memories, images, feelings, sentiments, meanings, and the work of the imagination. The feelings of a place are indeed the mental projections of individuals, but they come from collective experience and do not happen anywhere else. They belong to the place.' The geographer Edward Relph suggests that places are 'constructed in our memories and affections through repeated encounters and complex associations' and 'place experiences are necessarily time-deepened and memory qualified'.[27]

Churches, and often parish churches, because of their deep associations with an ancient past, and prominent positions in the geography of a place, are often the touch points for the memories of a given community. Buildings of this kind, especially because of the sense of their spiritual significance, help to anchor and shape the collective memories of given community. They act as the connecting point between past and present, between heaven and earth, between that which has been and that which might be.

Notes

1 David Goodhart suggests that three in five Britons live within 20 miles of where they lived when aged 14 but that few of these are graduates from Russell Group universities (David Goodhart, *The Road to Somewhere: The New Tribes Shaping British Politics*, 2nd edn (London: Penguin, 2017), p. xv). Churchgoers are disproportionately more likely to have gone to university. The question that I was asking was related to where people were born in relation to the immediate community in which they now live.

2 Andrew Menzies and Dean Phelan, *Kingdom Communities: Shining the Light of Christ Through Faith, Hope and Love* (Eugene, OR: Wipf and Stock, 2019), p. 40.

3 T. J. Gorringe, *A Theology of the Built Environment: Justice, Empowerment and Redemption* (Cambridge: Cambridge University Press, 2002), p. 1.

4 John Inge, *A Christian Theology of Place* (Aldershot: Ashgate, 2003), p. 5.

5 Andrew Rumsey, *Parish: An Anglican Theology of Place* (London: SCM Press, 2017), p. 11.

6 Rumsey, *Parish*, p. 11.

7 Walter Brueggemann, *The Land* (Philadelphia, PA: Fortress Press, 1977), p. 5.

8 Brueggemann, *Land*, p. 7.

9 Inge, *Place*, p. 40.

10 Brueggemann, *Land*, p. 3.

11 Brueggemann, *Land*, p. 4.

12 Inge, *Place*, p. 52.

13 Tom Wright, *Surprised by Hope* (London: SPCK, 2007).

14 Cited in Inge, *Place*, p. 10.

15 Inge, *Place*, p. 11.

16 Inge, *Place*, p. 18.

17 Michel de Certeau, 'Walking in the City', in Graham Ward (ed.), *The Certeau Reader* (Oxford: Blackwell, 2000), pp. 101–18.

18 De Certeau, 'Walking', p. 101.

19 De Certeau, 'Walking', p. 113.

20 De Certeau, 'Walking', p. 113.

21 Inge, *Place*, p. 83.

22 Clemens Sedmak, *Doing Local Theology: A Guide for Artisans of a New Humanity* (Maryknoll, NY: Orbis, 2002).

23 T. J. Gorringe, *Built Environment: Justice, Empowerment and Redemption* (Cambridge: Cambridge University Press, 2002), pp. 48–9.

24 Maurice Merleau-Ponty cited in Dan R. Stiver, *Theology after Ricoeur: New Directions in Hermeneutical Theology* (Louisville, KY: Westminster John Knox, 2001), p. 39.

25 Stiver, *Theology after Ricoeur*, p. 49.

26 Gorringe, *Built Environment*, p. 72.

27 Inge, *Place*, p. 84.

2

The Parish, its Future and its Present Crisis

When we talk about 'the parish' or 'a parish', what do we actually mean? The very fact that the concept and the concrete reality of parish life is a very long-established tradition that developed in different nations gradually and over a period of time means that we need to be careful about our description of the nature of a parish. Added to that, because it is a concept that is found in a number of ecclesial traditions – Anglican, Roman Catholic, Orthodox, the Church of Scotland and Lutheran, to name the better-known ones – also means that what we say about parish life in one place can be contradicted by understandings from another tradition and another nation. It is also true that the term 'parish' is used by some newer expressions of church – the Redeemed Christian Church of God being one example.

For the purposes of this book we are talking mainly about the United Kingdom and those nations that received concepts of 'parish' because of the missionary work that emanated from these four nations. Andrew Rumsey, in his book *Parish: An Anglican Theology of Place*, makes the point that the concept of parish 'finds its provenance in the integration of the Christian Church into the civic life of the Roman Empire.'[1]

Clearly, there were forms of organized church life that preceded that development. In the early life of the Church, Christianity was largely an urban phenomenon. Christianity was so identified with city or urban life that those outside these boundaries were described as the country folk or *pagani*. They were the people who often lived on the heath – heathens – and it was usually the task of the Church in the city to carry the gospel to these areas from the strength of the urban expression of Christianity.

In Britain, Celtic Christianity, following the Romano-Celtic civilization or in the areas of Britain and Ireland that had never been occupied by Roman power, often centred on the monasteries. Mission to surrounding areas was conducted from the centre of monastic life and influence.

The spread of organized parish life was gradual and was often associated with the organizing gift of the mission from Rome. Describing this process, Rumsey says:

> John Godfrey (1962, 1969) provides two useful surveys that focus on the Gregorian mission to England under Augustine and the role of his successor at Canterbury, Theodore of Tarsus (often credited with 'introducing' the parish to England), in implementing regional organization upon the hybrid of Roman and Celtic influences that formed the Anglo-Saxon Church before 'England' had any unified national identity. For Godfrey, the parochial idea as a 'local gathering' was so fundamental to the early Church that he can describe it as 'native to the Christian religion as such'.[2]

Even though this process began in the seventh century, Rumsey notes that:

> Nevertheless, many scholars of the English parish express reservation as to its origins and examination of its gradual establishment – a process that, by common recognition, did not form any coherent 'system' until the twelfth century – is made imprecise by the relative invisibility of the parish in historiography.[3]

Just as the development of the parish system is gradual, taking place over many centuries, so its purpose and function was also a complex matter. There are at least four key themes that help us to grapple with the complexity.

First, there is the extent to which a parish system, in its totality, helped to identify a sense of identity as a nation. The idea of the nation state is a relatively modern concept and clearly did not exist in the early centuries of the Christian mission in the British Isles. England was divided into a number of kingdoms, whose boundaries shifted in relation to the relative dominance of the kingdoms of the time. To make matters more complex, large parts of England were subject to the Danelaw and were certainly not part of the English political system. It was not until the period immediately prior to the Norman invasion that one could speak of a single political system in England.

But throughout the period from the commencement of both the Celtic and Roman missions until the Norman conquest, a period of more than 450 years, the work of mission had gradually extended the local reality of the parish – even if we perhaps might not yet call it a parish system as such. Following the settlement of the controversies between the Celtic and Roman missions at the Synod of Whitby in 664, it was possible to speak of the Church in England as one that operated as a single entity, certainly in terms of speaking for the Church in councils meeting outside England.

The Church was therefore sufficiently local, widespread and influential that it could convey a sense of what it meant to be English as being somehow identified with belonging to a Christian community that extended across the land. To that extent, the parish churches created a feeling of nationhood long before a political nation actually existed.

Following the Norman conquest, that degree of organization was extended, and in many cases the simpler and often wooden Saxon churches were replaced by larger stone churches. The vast cathedral structures, most of which survive to this day, together with the construction of many new monasteries, helped to complete the sense of an integrated society. It was in these early Norman times that we can begin to think of a parish system as compared with a parish presence. Being part of a single England, whether of Norman or Anglo-Saxon birth, was to be part of a Church that helped to preserve what it was to be English.

Second, the implication of the development of a 'system' – one might even say the *imposition* of a system – suggests a strong relationship with civil life. There is little doubt that the creation of bishops as 'princes' of the Church, living in bishops' palaces, mirrored the power of the state. This is not the place to argue about the extent to which the Church was involved in extending the power of the state or was able to mitigate the power of the state on behalf of the poor, but what we can say is that the relationship between Church and state undoubtedly impacts the role of the parish. The parish becomes the place where the reality of the national established Church is made present.

Whether that is the presence of the local church in providing schools that are connected to the parish, praying for the monarch and the government as part of the liturgy of an established Church, being connected to local government with such events as civil worship services, the presence of the national flag in parish churches, the proximity of the parish church to war memorials, the presence of the vicar at local civil occasions or many other local expressions of parish life unique to particular parishes, these and many other expressions of the connection between nationhood and local life are important.

Andrew Rumsey quotes the historian Adrian Hastings to illustrate the importance of this connection:

While not disputing the acceleration of national conscious-ness across Europe and the United States in the modern era, Hastings proceeds to demonstrate how, in England, this grew from an explicitly biblical narrative, without which the concept of nationhood *per se* simply would not exist. In this process, the creation of a national Church under Henry VIII and Elizabeth I may be viewed as giving particular political shape to an already long established self-perception.[4]

The point about that self-perception was that it was not primarily created by national institutions, though they undoubtedly reinforced such a structure. It required above all the presence of a local and visible reality to generate the self-perception. The visible presence of a significant building, usually in the physical centre of a given community, the presence of a priest and a local organized body of worshippers, gave shape and content to the sense of a Christian nation. To quote Andrew Rumsey once more:

> The vital counterpart to England's national formation was thus the development of a cohesive system of local communities, from whose varying Anglo-Saxon forms the parish gradually emerged as the principal one. However accurately or otherwise it was lodged in fact, Bede's *Ecclesiastical History* was instrumental in fixing the new national narrative that came to define Anglicanism ...
>
> The narrative synthesis Bede achieved was further fused by the Anglo-Saxon Chronicle, which plotted the points of national emergence by their relation to the commencement of the Christian era. When the English kingdoms became unified under King Alfred, not only were his foundations for common law prefaced with excerpts from the Mosaic Law ('modified for application to Christian nations'), but also his extension of civil society relied upon the 'parochial' bishops – as seen, for example, in their dissemination to local, secular leaders of Alfred's own translation of Pope Gregory's *Pastoral Care*.[5]

Third, the very close association between the parish church, and the parish with its clear boundaries, connected to specific villages and neighbourhoods, helped to give individual parishes a sense of their own local identity within a broader Christian framework. Andrew Rumsey cites a number of authors who point to the experience of the parish as representing a 'symbol of local belonging'.[6]

There are two key ideas that come together to enrich the idea of parish as embodying local identity. The first idea is the recovery of a theology of place. One of the leading studies in this area is John Inge's *A Christian Theology of Place*. This draws on the work of a number of authors who have asserted that the spaces we occupy, when vested with significance, become place as distinct from merely space. In this sense, the place in which we live and have our social relationships becomes the locale in which God meets us where we live. In this way, space is not just socially constructed but society becomes spatially constructed by means of the very local activities that help to make us human.

The second key idea that enriches the theoretical concept of space becoming place notes that this kind of construction occurs among the very ordinary activities of daily life. We eat together, we practise hospitality, we walk to known places in our neighbourhood. As we do so, we create and develop relationships within a rhythm of life.

That rhythm is reinforced by the activities of parish life, our worship, our regular meetings of one kind or another, the opportunities we have to serve and meet our neighbours. Each locale or parish has its own distinctive rhythms of life that create local identity and meaning. Local traditions are part of what makes a particular place somewhere that we love and value. Our neighbourhood is not just where we live, although it can be reduced to that, but it is part of a set of familiar relationships that are lived, felt and experienced. In this sense, the theology and theory of place – whether sacred or secular – is strengthened by local praxis.

John Inge centres a concern for place both in the Old Testament

Scriptures and in the writings of the New Testament. For Inge, it is the doctrine of the incarnation of Christ that causes us to insist on the importance of the local. Christ was profoundly located in a particular place and set of circumstances. The New Testament message makes little sense without a regard for the particularities of place.

At the end of his discussion of the fourth Gospel, W. D. Davies himself tells us that 'the Jesus of the fourth gospel is not a disincarnate spirit, but a man of flesh and blood who hungered and thirsted and was weary with his journey. His flesh was real flesh, and he was geographically conditioned as all men. But, although John presents us with itineraries of Jesus to some extent and although these were real, it was not the horizontal geographical movements that mattered to him. Rather, what was significant to John was the descent of Jesus from above, and his ascent thither. The fundamental spatial symbolism of the fourth gospel was not horizontal, but vertical'.

The vertical dimension is, of course, what Christians refer to as the incarnation, which is central to the New Testament witness and the Christian faith that springs from it, and the fact that Jesus was not a disincarnate spirit has profound implications. 'The Word became flesh,' St John tells us, 'and we have beheld his glory' (John 1.14). Thomas Torrance writes that the 'relation established between God and man in Jesus Christ constitutes Him as the place in all space and time where God meets with man in the actualities of human existence, and man meets with God and knows Him in His own divine Being'. It is in this that our hope is founded for 'unless the eternal breaks into the temporal and the boundless being of God breaks into the *spatial* existence of man and takes up dwelling within it, the vertical dimension vanishes out of a man's life and becomes quite strange to him – and man loses his place under the sun'. In their grappling with the significance of the New Testament material, the Church Fathers understood well that space and time had been 'Christified', to use Davies' term.[7]

The fourth theme that helps us to understand what we mean by parish relates to the way in which the ministry of the local parish is conceived. The parish does not exist to draw people into the Church, but is the means by which the message of the Church radiates outwards to seek to touch as many aspects of the parish as possible. In other words, the idea of the parish is not an inward movement that isolates people from the world but an outward movement that acts as the yeast that transforms the whole. The idea that the parish is there for the 'cure of souls' and that this influence is usually seen as a gradual process impacting the world outside of the confines of parish worship (an ideal that is not always clearly manifest) is an important element in understanding how the parish ought to operate. Parish boundaries, in the sense of knowing and interacting with that which lies within the parish, are therefore important in helping to shape the ministry and life of the local parish. Potentially these boundaries do not limit ministry so much as bring a focus to the content of ministry.

These four themes, therefore, bringing identity to the sense of being a nation prior to the creation of a nation state, anchoring and shaping relationships with civic life, helping to create local identity and attempting to give a particular focus and shape to ministry, help us to define what we mean when we use the term 'parish'. But this very definition helps us also to understand why there is a current sense of crisis for the parish system.

There are at least four major contributory factors that combine to produce immense pressure on the parish system. All four are part of long-term trends that have been in play for up to two centuries.

First is the impact of immense population shifts since the Agrarian and Industrial Revolution. Arguably, population shifts have taken place for as long as people have inhabited the land. Some have been dramatic and sudden – for example, the arrival of the plague in medieval times. The impact of the plague was sometimes to eradicate whole communities and even today it is possible to identify parish churches that stand alone in countryside where no homes exist. These can be a visible reminder of the devastating impact of disease and death on particular villages and rural communities.

In more recent times the shifts in population have been primarily from the countryside to the city in the late eighteenth and nineteenth centuries and then from the inner city to the suburbs after the Second World War. That second movement from the cities to surrounding communities has been accompanied by shifts from the north to the south, and particularly the south-east of England. In addition, cities across the British Isles have experienced significant migration, primarily of those who, for a variety of reasons, have chosen to live in the inner-city areas.

The parish system, as it developed over the course of at least a millennium, was particularly well suited to serve a rural-based population. The emphasis was on covering the whole land with boundaries that reflected the working pattern and lives of those who worked the land. Following the Agrarian Revolution, beginning in the mid-eighteenth century, far fewer workers were required to work on the farms. That process has continued almost until the present day.

The revolution in farming practices was accompanied very soon afterwards by the Industrial Revolution, which demanded new workers in the mills, factories, shipyards, railways, canals and coalmines of the economy. Some very small towns soon became huge cities. The city of Leeds would be a good example of that process.

The Anglican Church was very slow to adapt to this new reality. For example, in Leeds, despite the huge growth of the population and the expansion of housing to accommodate it, for many decades there was still only one parish to serve the new city. That pattern was repeated across England and it was not really until the latter half of the nineteenth century that the Church of England saw the need for the creation of new parishes and the accompanying construction of new parish church buildings.

A trend develops of the depopulation of the countryside with its traditional links to particular localities and traditions attached to parish life, and the growth of cities with an insufficient parish structure to accommodate the new arrivals. Non-conformist churches were far quicker to adapt to this new situation. The late eighteenth century and early nineteenth century revivals began as a religious revival within the Anglican tradition through the work of John Wesley and George Whitefield but they did not remain that way. As the non-conformists, particularly the Methodists, but also the many new denominations that emerged in the revivals, grew and began new churches, so the claim of the Anglican Church to be the National Church was somewhat weakened, partly by its lack of presence but also because of the loss of people.

The later recovery of the Church of England, in the latter part of the nineteenth century, together with the growth of the population as a whole, meant that some of the loss of prestige and position was ameliorated by the early part of the twentieth century. But other disturbing patterns were emerging.

In particular, it became clear that the Church of England was significantly distanced from the working classes, who were almost certainly connected with the Anglican Church while they were living as agricultural workers in the pre-industrial era. But either they, or their children or their grandchildren, did not make that vital connection once they had left their rural context.

In the initial phases of the move to the cities, the revival movement impacted the cities just as it had some rural communities. Working-class communities were reached and helped in their attempts to make their new life in an urban environment bearable. The congregation became the place where working-class leaders could be formed, where children and adults could receive a basic education and, more importantly, attain the life skills that would enable them to advance. The process of 'redemption and lift' often meant that the children and the grandchildren of those working-class parents who embraced Christianity in its revival fervour had often moved out of their working-class occupations to become doctors, lawyers, teachers and business people.

The result was that by the end of the nineteenth century, churches fairly widely saw that the working class was significantly alienated from the churches. Church life was increasingly a middle-class and a suburban affair. The Church of England, as much as the new non-conformist denominations, thrived in these middle-class settings.

There were numerous attempts made to reach the working classes with the good news of the gospel. Sometimes these were local or regional and sometimes they had a national significance. The Oxford Movement within the Anglican Church appealed to graduates from Oxford University in particular to offer themselves as clergy dedicated to work in those poorer areas of English cities where others were not inclined to serve. Bishop Lightfoot in Durham, working more with evangelical clergy, had a group of enthusiastic recruits willing to go anywhere at the bishop's bidding. They were called Lightfoot's Lambs. 'Anywhere' often meant working with the poor.

The Methodist Church developed a system of Central Halls, designed to reach the working class. Various city missions, notably London City Mission, deliberately targeted working-class districts, attempting to recruit mission workers for every street in some areas. To a large extent, the Salvation Army was brought into being to reach those in poorer neighbourhoods. At a slightly later period, Pentecostals began with a similar concern and impact.

The result of all this activity, at least for the Anglican Church, meant that parishes in poorer areas struggled to be effective in reaching out to the large working-class populations living within their parish boundaries. When, after the Second World War, slum redevelopment resulted in the creation of large working-class estates, often on the edge of towns and cities, the problem was compounded.

One parish in Birmingham with a population of close to 20,000 has an attendance at the main service on a Sunday of less than 100. Most of those who attend come from the part of the parish that is middle class. Efforts to work with the large working-class populations living on the estates within the parish have largely failed. Parishes such as these have experienced the pressure of maintaining a sense of serving the whole community long before such pressures have impacted other kinds of parish settings.

At the same time that parishes with large populations of white working-class parishioners have experienced difficulty in conducting effective ministry, many churches in inner-city areas have experienced the phenomenon of large-scale immigration from populations that are committed to religions other than Christianity. Putting into practice the ideal of the 'cure of souls' in such situations has been, and remains, difficult. Some parishes have had no choice but to merge with nearby parishes, with church closures and subsequent sales of prominent buildings adding to the sense of a crisis for the Church in these areas.

All of these difficulties among specific parishes have come alongside the general decline in church attendance across the British Isles as a whole. This overall drop in attendance has been accompanied by a decline in all of the traditional functions of the Church – attendance at Sunday schools, church weddings, funerals and christenings. With less than 2.5 per cent of the population attending an Anglican church on a Sunday morning, it is hard to maintain the sense that this is the national, established Church operating in every part of the nation through a parish system.

The decline in attendance, and so in finance, has made it increasingly difficult for many parish churches to operate effectively in the attempt to reach out from the worshipping community to the broader population in the parish. Smaller numbers have often meant that parishes have been required to group together and to share a priest with a number of other parishes. Not that this situation is always negative. One study of the growth and decline of churches in a particular diocese noted that a good deal of growth had occurred in parish churches that had lost their full-time clergy person.

This overall decline, coupled with the reality that congregations often consist of a much older age profile than the broader population in the parish, can produce something of a siege mentality. Once that occurs, the possibility of introducing new initiatives, especially around mission, becomes instead a concern to survive. In such a scenario the ideal of the parish collapses and it can feel that a small clique, unrepresentative of the broader community, maintains control and – however inadvertently – operates to keep newcomers as precisely that: people who do not belong.

To all of this difficulty is added the reality that we described in Chapter 1: the mobility of populations. The ability of parishioners to travel to neighbouring parishes produces a situation where there is an element of consumer choice. Potential worshippers are no longer bound by parish loyalties but feel free to attend churches that are apparently more successful, or who offer a form of worship and broader ethos that is more in keeping with the preferences of individual parishioners. Some parish churches are perceived to be more successful and can act inadvertently as competitors, undermining the ministry and life of parishes nearby. In such a situation it can feel as if the whole system of parish life becomes more like that of a series of gathered congregations, mirroring the theory and practice of non-conformist denominations and networks. While the diocese can be grateful to the few larger congregations in the system, who contribute disproportionately to the finances of the diocese as a whole, it becomes an increasing struggle to maintain the system of parish life in its entirety.

It is all too easy to feel that denominations that are committed to a parish system are in reality becoming more like non-conformist churches working with a gathered church model. However, such a conclusion is rather too simplistic because, strangely, denominations with a gathered church model also operate more of a parish mentality than is sometimes recognized. Many non-conformist congregations have a strong sense of the context in which they are located.

They may not use the language of parish, but nevertheless they have a strong sense of the 'patch' that they view as their primary area of ministry. That conscious or unconscious perspective is often reinforced by particular physical features – a recognized area of town or city, a neighbourhood defined not by parish boundaries but by the existence of major roads, the impact of other factors such as the presence of schools, factories, shops, hospitals and the reality of very local patterns of belonging and social activity.

The idea of reconnecting with a particular neighbourhood, of seeking to 'join God in the neighbourhood', of becoming much more sensitive to the needs of the immediate community, is a growing theme in the recovering sense of ministry among such denominations and networks. They may not have a sense of covering the whole of a nation with a network of churches, but the lived reality feels more like the idea of a parish church than is sometimes recognized.

What might be emerging, regardless of a commitment to a parish system as such, is a situation where larger churches in a given area act effectively as 'resource' churches willing to invest heavily in their immediate context but also generous in terms of helping other congregations, either by seeking to re-plant congregations that are failing, or by beginning new congregations or simply by seeking to offer resources to churches that are struggling. In such a scenario, mission is often the driver to cause churches to connect with one another, regardless of denominational affiliation, to produce an effective local presence and so to strengthen the Church overall. The crisis of the parish may be forcing a re-evaluation of how mission in local areas is actually conceived.

Notes

1 Andrew Rumsey, *Parish: An Anglican Theology of Place* (London: SCM Press, 2017), p. 8.

2 Rumsey, *Parish*, p. 8.

3 Rumsey, *Parish*, p. 8.

4 Rumsey, *Parish*, pp. 98f.

5 Rumsey, *Parish*, pp. 99f.

6 Rumsey, *Parish*, p. 12.

7 See John Inge, *A Christian Theology of Place* (Ashgate, 2003), p. 51; emphasis original.

3

Parish as a Healthy Place

Amid the many difficulties faced by churches throughout the Western world, two apparently contradictory realities strike seasoned observers of the overall ecclesial scene. First, in the remarkable words of Loren Mead, church decline is not necessarily something that local leaders can seriously affect. In other words, something is happening in the broader culture that is producing a long-term tendency towards the decline of the Church, thus sharpening the crisis of the parish.

Second, some congregations are growing. Is it the case that these growing congregations trace their growth to an exceptional set of circumstances? Are they all located in suburban areas? Do they grow only because their resource base enables them to attract worshippers from neighbouring areas? Are they in such unusual situations that they cannot be replicated elsewhere and therefore do not offer transferable insights? The answer to all of these questions may be yes, and yet there are sufficient indications of healthy, growing churches in a wide variety of contexts that there almost certainly are lessons that can be learnt.

So how do we reconcile these two contrasting realities – overall decline in the face of a huge cultural shift, and evidence that despite this hostile environment growth is still possible? The answer does not lie in the adoption of a set of techniques, methods and programmes. That does not mean that such technical ingredients have no value, but it does mean that their value is related to something that operates at a deeper level.

Church health does not come about by measuring specific 'health factors', useful though that might be as an indicator of the extent of the task. Rather, it lies in the capacity to actually create health, which is different from simply measuring it.

The crisis facing us lies in the painful reality that our changed context means that the skills, priorities, processes and gifts required to produce a healthy parish have shifted enormously. It requires a different imagination to produce a healthy parish life in the current context than it did, probably as recently as the 1950s. My father was a clergyman in the 1950s, and in that period nearly all of the churches in the Scottish town where he worked could be described as healthy.

To a large extent, Christendom still existed, which essentially meant that the overwhelming majority of the population regarded themselves as Christians. They could tell you what church they belonged to even if they rarely attended. The church was regarded as an essential and desirable part of the community. Religious Instruction (not religious education) was taken seriously in all schools, and clergy were present in all of the secular institutions–either as chaplains or as welcome guests.

To be a healthy parish in those circumstances required three basic functions. Worship services needed to be properly conducted, pastoral visiting had to be thorough, and a pattern of programmes designed to meet the needs of particular groups (such as children and young people) needed to be effectively operated. If these elements were in place, then provided the clergyperson leading them was reasonably personable in their normal human relationships, then parish or congregational life tended to be both healthy and very local in its impact.

The present post-Christendom context has created a mission field that few church leaders are trained and equipped to understand. If that is the situation for leaders, it is even more the case for church members. The reality is that the creation of parish and congregational health in a mission situation requires a very different skill set and approach.

There is no single factor that is more or less important than others. Instead, there is a necessity to create a complex fabric that is much more about the creation of a certain kind of community than it is about the implementation of programmes, even mission programmes. I want to suggest that there are at least eight elements that need to be explored and developed in the creation of healthy community. We might call these elements 'practices'.

1 The sense of God as agent

In *Practices for the Refounding of God's People: The Missional Challenge of the West*, Alan Roxburgh and I explore the extent to which the culture of the Enlightenment, which has produced modernity, has made us all functional atheists. In other words, although we may believe in God, and may even have been profoundly impacted and changed by experiences of God, nevertheless there is a deep sense that man, not God, is the agent that changes matters. Even though we ask for God's help, in our imagination it is 'we' who are entrusted by God to take the initiative.

We write in the book:

The welfare state, while rooted in Christian imagination, illustrated how the secular state had taken the place of church and local communities to become the primary space for the care and support of citizens. Care became managed and bureaucratized through state legislation and public policy. By means of taxation, state-run safety nets protected citizens from the worst effects of the invisible hand. Churches were increasingly relegated to the care of the private, inner lives of those citizens who chose spiritual succor. From the perspective of 2017 this story now seems a strange, alien world but it was the one that shaped the stories of success, class and economic progress which still infuse our imagination. Within this story it would be the state that stepped in to provide the support systems for social life. The primary unit of social life would now be shifted from what had been understood as neighborhood to that of the state and its apparatus for looking after people.

In this period Protestant denominations fully structured themselves around the hub–spoke organization that ran the dominant business organizations of the day. These organizations were run by centralized managers and professionals resourcing local congregations. As managed care through professionals became the norm, the churches followed suit in the training of the clergy and denominational leadership. While the churches were invited to provide ameliorating programs for people in need, their basis reality was clear – their role in the postwar era had radically changed. The churches were now *useful adjuncts* to the liberal state and a capitalist economy. State and the market were the overarching framers and sponsors of social life. The market now provided a brief, golden age of goods-and-services and full employment. It offered the means for individuals to make their own private lives. It was as if, with the end of war, the promise of Modernity's Wager had finally become available for everyone as the new middle class took its place at the center of this society.[1]

The shift of gravity involved in the creation of what has sometimes been called 'Modernity's Wager' – the idea that life can be good without God – has diminished our public sense of God and his agency. It is difficult to imagine mission, or healthy Christian community, without a much more deeply rooted sense of God in our midst.

But creating a deep sense of God as the initiator of mission is not easily done against the backdrop of a culture that pushes us in the opposite direction. We are not only seeking to engage in mission in such a setting, we are also unconsciously shaped by – we might even say 'evangelized by' – that same culture. It is not sufficient to simply state that we want God to be central to our life and thinking, it has to become a shared experience. It requires considerable faith, courage and imagination to begin to create a culture of that kind.

Some congregations have been helped in this process by contact with Christians from other continents, places where the sense of God as agent has not been eroded by the culture of the Enlightenment. Even where congregations are primarily composed of white European or North American peoples, the development of relationships with individual Christians and congregations that are formed from a different imagination can help us to re-experience that which previous generations would have taken for granted. God is not just there to assist our ambitions for growth and health. We need to be deeply grounded in a spirituality that draws us to a profound awareness of the presence of God, learning to listen to the priorities that God brings to our ability to see his hand at work in our everyday life.

2 Expectant worship

When my wife and I began ministry in inner-city Birmingham, several decades ago, we were met with a largely elderly, loyal and determined congregation who certainly felt that they were under siege. The high fences that protected the car park, the huge gates that kept it locked, and the barbed wire on the roof were all suggestive of the pressure and isolation that this congregation exuded.

Not surprisingly, the worship experience was not wonderful. The weekly services were certainly consistent: mostly competently conducted, predictable and frankly rather dull. I had to wonder whether I would be prepared to invite anyone to worship in that situation.

After a few years of activity, the church became rather full, new people had come and the worship experience had somehow been transformed. I deliberately say 'the worship experience' because the form of worship was completely unchanged and yet somehow everything had changed. I began to reflect on what precisely it was that was different. Obviously, a full church changed the dynamics but that was not what was going on here.

I finally came to believe that the essential difference was that sense that somehow God was here. Of course, I don't mean to suggest that God was absent previously – deliberately avoiding our place of worship in former times. And yet the sense of expectation, that God was going to speak, to act to impact those who came, was palpable and of course very welcome.

How had that happened? That was more difficult to explain and in some ways I couldn't explain it; I could only observe that it was so. I was certainly not in a position to analyse the situation and market a new programme more widely. I could only be grateful to God for what had happened.

There is an inevitable tension between the simple fact that liturgy (and we all have liturgies of one kind or another whether written or extemporary) is a drama – and therefore performance of one kind or another is involved. And yet if worship is reduced to a performance, then somehow it ceases to be worship. I recall a few years ago attending a church where the very loud worship band played songs that very few seemed to know, or indeed could sing. At a certain point the lead singer yelled at the congregation, 'sing, church, sing'. It was very hard to see how they could meaningfully participate in what had become just a performance. Instead, the congregation simply stood, largely silent, and waited for the singing to end.

At a very deep level, the call to worship is not primarily directed towards the congregation, though of course that is part of the intention, but it is also a call, a plea to God for him to be present. For worship to be worship, God needs to be present; whether in word or sacrament, fellowship or prayer, we need that sense that God is here for worship to satisfy the soul.

The process of creating an expectancy around worship

cannot be reduced to a formula. It takes time, patience, not a little skill, and the creation of hope. Hope-filled congregations tend to develop the faith that leads to an expectancy that God is present and is going to act in ways that we may not understand but we can begin to apprehend if not comprehend. We centre ourselves in God and in the relationships of trust and love that hope-filled congregations are capable of developing over time.

3 Leadership

What makes an effective leader? Are leaders born or made? What is it that causes people to follow some people but not others, whether they hold an office of leadership or not? What is it that inspires trust and confidence? Whole books are devoted to this topic and we can only take a few lines to describe the kind of leader who is able to create a healthy parish or congregational life.

In the absence of more space, I want to highlight four key areas that leaders need to consider.

Character as more important than skills

Skills and competencies derived from a mixture of natural gifting, personality, training and life experience are understandably valued in leading any institution in challenging and complex times. But it is noticeable that the New Testament gives a higher priority to character than to skills.

There are no shortcuts to the building of good character. This is the challenge for all Christians, not just leaders. It can help to have had good mentors while growing up, and it is valuable for leaders to retain trusted mentors and friends around them to offer the difficult words of advice and direction that only those who love us can bring. Who are these people in your life?

The goal is to be more Christ-like, to put in place a rhythm of prayer, retreat, reflection, listening, friendships and times of rest that act as a foundation for the building of character. These disciplines are never a substitute or a guarantee that good character will result, but the ingredients help.

Consistency as a fundamental pillar in building trust

People tend to trust leaders who stick to their word, who keep their promises, whose words are matched by deeds, and who demonstrate that they can be trusted. Simple actions such as not continually cancelling meetings, being present when you have said you will be there, are important. Being on time (or even a few minutes early) sends silent signals that you are trustworthy.

That does not mean that leaders cannot make mistakes. Of course that will happen, but in a healthy parish, mistakes are quickly forgiven and forgotten. But frequent errors sometimes reflect a more chaotic lifestyle: an inability to set good priorities and stick with them, and not to be blown about by every new opinion that comes along. Trust is hard to earn and all too easy to lose. It's a precious commodity.

Love being more important than power and authority

Particularly in the worlds of business and politics but more widely in secular life, leadership is associated with power and authority, and possibly even a degree of ruthlessness. Jesus is very clear that the kind of combative, competitive attitude that leads to a concern for power and position is not how leaders in the kingdom of God should operate. He not only tackled that question very directly, but he then demonstrated servant leadership in the washing of the feet of those who had been demanding power and authority just a few hours previously. Love, grace, kindness, and patience should characterize those who seek to lead. That is easy to say but hard to practise, when dealing with the pressures that leaders face.

The business consultant John Blakey, in his book *The Trusted*

Executive: Nine Leadership Habits that Inspire Results, Relationships and Reputation, has this to say about love, or kindness/benevolence as he sometimes expresses it:

> We show our good wishes to others through care, generosity and kindness. I have been in many a boardroom where the leader has publicly humiliated a member of the team through put-downs, sarcasm and withering personal criticism. The leaders were highly able and as honest as the day is long, but they were not trusted. We could get away with that in the blue pill world because we used authority as a surrogate for trust. Increasingly, this approach will not work in a world where transparency dissolves the traditional levers of authority ...
> Executive leaders who focus on building ability, integrity and benevolence in parallel are practising trustworthy leadership. In focusing on the three pillars we work equally hard to develop our ability to deliver results, our integrity to 'walk the talk' and our benevolence to do well to others.[2]

The priority of a healthy personal spiritual life

One of the problems that leaders face is that tyranny of the diary, the demand to fit ever more meetings, events and preparation into an already full schedule. People can be very demanding of our time while giving little thought to what that might mean for the leader concerned. In the midst of these pressures, what tends to suffer is the leader's personal spiritual life. Times of retreat are cancelled or never made, personal prayer becomes ever shorter. It is very difficult to maintain the kind of structures that allow our spiritual life to remain healthy, and yet this is the very wellspring of leadership. We could almost say it is what allows us to operate as a leader at all.

4 Team and gift mix

Leadership is never about one person, it is about a team. Yes, there may be a team leader and it is also possible that the team leader is paid and others are not, but leadership is still about a team. Even if a ministry situation begins with a single leader, the goal is always to build a team.

There are many types of team and there are many ways of exercising team leadership. Some leaders work better from a more participative or consultative style while others prefer a more directive approach. There is no right or wrong approach; different contexts demand a variety of approaches, just as different personalities work better with one approach rather than another.

What matters is that the team agrees and understands the ground rules with which the team is working. It is also vital that the team attempts to include a range of gifts within itself. There are many tools to assess the gifts that could be in a team. We can use the APEPT model, the Belbin model, the Strength-finders model, or many more. In addition, it is helpful for teams to understand both the nature of the gifts in the team and also how the personalities of its members impact styles of communication that often filter the ways in which each individual interacts with other members. Again, there is a wide range of tools available to help with the process of discovery. That could be anything from Myers Briggs, to DISC or the Enneagram test.

Whatever language we use, a good team must include diverse gifts, be capable of understanding how those gifts work together, and at least include some entrepreneurial as well as some pastoral elements in the mix. This all takes time, but healthy teams need to invest time, especially in the phase of their early formation. Part of that time is invested in work and some in having fun together.

5 The ministry of the people of God

Churches often talk about the 'priesthood of all believers', recognizing that all are gifted, that all have a calling to serve, and that participation in some kind of ministry is a fundamental part of the creation of a healthy Christian community. That is the theory and most leaders and congregations will give some assent to it. But the reality is much more often the 80/20 rule – 80 per cent of the work undertaken by 20 per cent of the congregation. Studies have demonstrated that where the 80/20 rule applies, little if any growth takes place. Conversely, when congregations produce a situation where at least 50 per cent are actively involved in some kind of ministry, then growth is almost inevitable. In other words, healthy parish life is participatory parish life.

One of the challenges of leading others is the simple fact that, in the short term at least, it is far easier (and quicker) to do things yourself. Developing others takes time, patience and skill. One writer has described this tension as the difference between telling the time and building a clock. His illustration suggests that if someone asks you the time you can potentially tell them the time on every occasion that they ask you. But another solution would be to help them build or acquire their own timepiece. Building the clock requires much more up-front time but in the long run it is a more effective piece of empowerment.

Leaders need to ask themselves, 'Is the core task of leadership to do or to cause to be done?' If it is the latter, then leaders (or leadership teams) are called to the costly and time-consuming task of empowering others – and that always begins by helping to locate the passion and calling of those we seek to serve.

On one occasion I asked a leader what he had done to take a church that had been stuck for ten years with a large membership of 1,000 people, and move it over a fairly short period of time to a membership of many thousands. He told me about three key elements in his initial approach, the most important of which was a 'piece of empowerment'. He had noticed that participation in ministry was low and yet this was a congregation with many talented people.

He located 100 men and women in the church who attended regularly, who seemed to have a strong Christian commitment, and yet who were not involved in anything beyond Sunday worship. He laid on a meal and asked those present to express their dreams. 'If you could do anything in terms of Christian ministry, what would that be?' he asked. He also accompanied that question with a dangerous promise: 'If you can express your dream I promise that the church will do everything it can to empower that possibility.' It was a turning point for the church. Huge amounts of energy were released, most of which were focused on the community in which the church was located.

6 People of peace

The term 'people of peace' has been fairly widely used in evangelistic or mission circles over the last decade or so. We can also use the term 'gatekeepers' to describe what we mean. People of peace relates to the sending out of the 70 in Luke 10, specifically to the instruction of Jesus to declare peace to the house of those who gave the disciples a welcome.

I first came across a contemporary application of this passage in the context of evangelistic work and church planting in India. Church planters were instructed to look for 'people of peace' as the ones who would provide a breakthrough in the new village or communities into which they were entering.

Having thought about such an application, I began to realize that I had witnessed just such a phenomenon in my own experience of evangelism and church planting. Specifically, in the first full-time ministry undertaken by my wife and I, in inner-city Birmingham, we were initially unsure how to connect with the immediate neighbourhood. There were no natural connections. No one who was a member of the church lived in the area, no one who lived in the area had any connection with the church. There were no community programmes, nothing that could even lead to a conversation, still less a conversion! How to break through was a question constantly on our minds.

After some time we decided to go door to door and offer a home study programme on the person of Jesus. It was a kind of Alpha course before Alpha was invented and marketed. To our amazement, in the first 100 homes that we visited, 20 people expressed interest, 12 actually came, and six people made commitments and were subsequently baptized.

Reflecting on the success of the programme we later realized that this success was not so much due to the programme itself, but to the home that was offered as the place where we might meet. The home was occupied by a person of peace in that neighbourhood. That reality made it a safe place to come and explore.

Mobilizing a significant percentage of people in the worshipping community into some kind of ministry creates a strong possibility that people of peace in the neighbourhood will be contacted. These relationships represent the breakthrough friendships that help to bring fresh streams of hope and experience into the life of the parish.

7 Community connectedness (God is there ahead of us)

Looking for people of peace contains the inherent conviction that the God of mission is already at work in the wider parish or community in which our worshipping community is located.

In the context of Christendom, the focus of parish life is often the worshipping community and the programmes that are operated from that base. In a post-Christendom context, the natural connections that have existed for many years have been deeply fractured. The normal interactions of christenings, marriages, funerals and routine pastoral contact have become fractured. Waiting for people to come to us no longer produces

43

fruit, no matter how good our programmes might be. That is not to suggest that none of these interactions take place, but rather that they have become much diminished. Those who still come tend to be those who are already Christians and who are actively searching for a spiritual home.

Looking for the places where God is at work is usually unfamiliar territory for us, and initial attempts to reach into the community may not produce instant results. We will make mistakes and it requires a good deal of patience to listen carefully for those places where God is already at work.

One very ambitious church planter told me that he moved to a new area and built friendships among those who were not Christians. After relationships had been established and once his intention to plant a church became known, conversations turned to where this church was going to be located, what it might look like, and how he was going to go about his task. After a time, he took the unusual step of inviting a group of those with whom trust had been established and suggesting that those who were taking part in the conversation help him to imagine what a church that they might attend could look like. These were the people who began to form the church. God is at work in our neighbourhoods – the question is what he is doing and with whom.

Another missioner was appointed by a denomination to work for three years with those who were not part of any existing congregation. The challenge was to spend the first year listening to what God was doing, then on the basis of what was learnt to launch an experiment. At the end of three years, the experiment resulted in a worshipping group that consisted of those who had never ventured near any existing church. Not only was this group larger than the attendance of any nearby church, but the demographic – notably a much younger age group – made up the new worshipping community. The natural links of this group into the community were much greater than those who attended existing churches but had become somewhat isolated from the wider community – or parish in this case – that they desired to serve.

8 A culture of welcome

The development of worshipping communities with strong, natural links to the wider community, such that it becomes easier for people to enter a place of worship, will hopefully develop a culture of welcome. That is more than offering a warm welcome when people arrive, encouraging as this might be. It extends to the many opportunities that are created for people to talk together, to meet in a variety of settings and activities, to eat together perhaps and basically to develop a sense of belonging well before a commitment to become a Christian or to commit to some kind of formal membership takes place. In the words of some thinkers, these are places with 'fuzzy' boundaries rather than sharply defined ones.

These are not easy cultures to develop and maintain, but it is much more likely if significant numbers within the church are already mobilized. It also illustrates why it is so difficult to renew existing churches without recruiting a significant number of people who will help to develop a new kind of culture within the congregation.

None of these elements constitute a formula or a model. No single element is more important than another. Each reinforces the others. Rarely can this approach to bringing about health happen quickly, but it is possible – and significant numbers of churches are finding precisely that.

Some years ago I visited a church that was the result of three churches, all located close to one another, uniting to form a single congregation. As a result of the merger they had an excellent re-modelled building and a congregation that filled the available space. The overwhelming majority of the congregation was over 60 years of age. These were three congregations that 50 or so years ago had been relatively healthy and vibrant.

I asked the leaders what was new in terms of mission. They told me that they were now running a café church once a month. I asked whether anyone new had come as a result. They told me that, to their surprise, no one new had come. 'We were told that this was the latest thing and that if we did this it would be effective in reaching new people.'

This was a sobering moment. I was witnessing reliance on a model without any of the culture change that we have described in this chapter. These were delightful people – committed and friendly – but it is likely that unless culture change takes place, this strategically placed congregation will not exist in 20 years' time.

Notes

1 Alan J. Roxburgh and Martin Robinson, *Practices for the Refounding of God's People: The Missional Challenge of the West* (New York: Church Publishing, 2018), pp. 58f.

2 John Blakey, *The Trusted Executive: Nine Leadership Habits that Inspire Results, Relationships, and Reputation* (London: Kogan Page, 2016), pp. 44f.

4

Presence in the Inner City

The story of the relationship between Christianity and the city is a complex one and this is not a book that is primarily about the history of that relationship. However, there are two important points to note in order to set a context for our later discussion of the Church in the inner city.

First, as Graham Ward suggests:

> The Bible is ambivalent towards cities. The first cities were built by men of demonstrable power and ambition. Cain, having murdered his brother Abel and being informed by God that he would be a vagabond all this life, 'built a city, and called the name of the city after the name of his son, Enoch' (Genesis 4:17). The origins of the city, for the Bible, seem to lie in masculine expressions of defiance, insecurity, the need to find substitutions and consolations for the loss of God, and the desire to take the place of that God, to become a dynasty.[1]

At the beginning of the story of the people of Israel, Abram leaves the city and becomes a wandering nomad. Even the construction of Jerusalem carries a mixed message. On the one hand it was a holy place, the location of the temple and of pilgrimage, yet on the other hand it was to be destroyed. Although Christians are called to be citizens, that call is to be citizens of heaven, and not of any earthly city.

Yet despite this ambivalence, Christianity as it developed

over the first 500 years was primarily an urban faith. Those who lived in the countryside (the *pagani*) were unlikely to have been evangelized – they were pagans in both senses of the word. In England, country dwellers were outsiders who lived on the heath – again, very literally, heathens.

Yet all that was to change once the countryside became the primary source of wealth and prosperity and Christianity successfully engaged with the rural context, particularly through the parish system. Monastic life, the primary means of evangelism in the Dark Ages, largely operated in relationship with the rural context, not the city. Towns and cities learnt to serve the needs of the surrounding countryside, whereas, arguably, rural life had previously functioned to serve the needs of the city.

Second, the relationship of the Church to cities is further complicated by the way in which cities subsequently develop. Graham Ward goes on to describe three huge phases of the development of the city in the Western world after the close of the Dark Ages.[2] He notes that the first phase, dating from the early Renaissance period, was dominated by merchants and bankers. This was a mercantile city that produced commodities, serviced international trade, and even sponsored a limited form of industrialization. These wealthy centres once again came to dominate the countryside that lay around them. While these cities became wealthy, they nevertheless operated on what we might call a human scale that enabled the Church to serve the distinct communities that had begun to evolve in this first phase.

The second phase began, as we have seen, with the Industrial Revolution, which occurred in the various parts of the Western world at different times, but began in England in the mid to late eighteenth century. This form of the city, as the term Industrial Revolution suggests, carried with it new demands for production. The social impact of this second phase was to generate new cities, to dramatically grow existing cities, and to create a new mobility in the population, as those who formerly lived in the countryside moved to the city. That process continues today on a global scale. It is estimated that sometime in the first three decades of the twenty-first century the majority of people in the world will live in cities.

In this second phase, workers lived close to their places of work, often in housing built by the factory owners. During this period, suburbia begins to develop as a means of enabling the middle classes to live outside the city itself. To a certain extent, suburbia seeks to re-create an experience of the rural within the framework of a larger city. That development was enabled by the creation of different forms of transport, particularly the railway system, which made it possible to commute between the workplace and home.

It became obvious to Christian leaders that something had decisively shifted in the relationship between the newly arrived working classes and the Church. The dramatic growth of the cities produced a crisis for the Church of England, primarily because the parish system did not expand sufficiently quickly to take account of the population growth. *Faith in the City* identifies three issues in this developing crisis.[3]

First, the Anglican Church failed to provide sufficient church buildings or clergy: 'As early as 1736 in Sheffield and 1751 in Leeds, local clergy were complaining that the lack of churches encouraged the growth of non-conformity and even non-churchgoing.'[4]

Second, an obvious alienation between middle-class Anglicanism and the working classes had developed: 'the 1851 census showed that, in the 36 registration districts of London, total Anglican attendances varied from 57 per cent of the population in suburban Hampstead (which was very high, even by rural standards) to 6 per cent in Shoreditch.'[5]

Third, there was evidence of a growth in anti-clericalism among the emerging working-class urban dwellers: 'The Church of England was viewed by many as being aligned with the powerful and the privileged. But there also existed a secularist element in the working class, which had an influence out of proportion to its numbers because so many secularists were active in politics or trade unions.'[6]

The initial experience of the non-conformists in the life of the growing cities was somewhat different from that of the Anglicans. As suggested above, the absence of Anglican buildings contributed to the development of non-conformist activity, particularly because they were active in church planting (or chapel building). The leadership of these new congregations was often drawn from the people they were trying to reach. In addition, the range of their activities offered dignity, hope and personal development for the members of these new congregations.

Non-conformists, through their Sunday schools, their preaching classes, the development of leadership training, especially through their small-group system, and the creation of social activities for all ages in the congregation, enabled a level of participation that generated a sense that these churches stood at the heart of communities that had few other social amenities. Although it is true that secularists were very involved in politics and the trade unions, it is also the case that the non-conformist churches developed leaders who were very active in these areas of national life.

However, this more hopeful relationship between vibrant and growing non-conformity and the growing working classes in the industrial landscape of Western countries was not always capable of being maintained. The primary reason for this difficulty lay in the often described phenomenon of 'redemption and lift'. The children and grandchildren of working people, often through the values and disciplines learnt in the chapels that they frequented, became doctors, lawyers, teachers, accountants and successful entrepreneurs. In other words, they often joined the middle classes, and so not only moved from the inner-city areas, but also deprived the congregations that their parents and grandparents had initiated of ongoing gifted leadership. Although this was ameliorated to some extent by the development of new movements among the working classes, such as the Salvation Army and the Pentecostals, the same phenomenon was usually repeated in these newer denominations.

The Anglicans managed to make some recovery in the second half of the nineteenth century. The realization that new parishes and parish churches needed to be developed and that suitable clergy needed to be recruited, allowed the Church of England to expand their presence in the newly created cities and expanded industrial towns of England. The Oxford Movement, with its laudable commitment to ministry among the poor, and equivalent evangelical movements, brought a new vigour and enthusiasm to ministry among working-class people. The benefit was the reality of presence on the ground – a realistic parish system. The weakness remained the sense of social distance between those who ministered and those who were being ministered to.

So far I have not mentioned the Roman Catholic presence in the urban areas of the city. It was not possible to build Catholic places of worship until the law changed in 1829. Part of the reason for the change in legislation was simply the arrival of large numbers of Irish Catholics as workers, first on the canals and roads, second in the factories and later in building the railways.

That social reality, that the Catholic Church was dominated by largely Irish Catholic communicants, created a genuine Christian presence on the ground in the inner city, one that was to last for many years. That strength has continued, partly because of growing waves of immigration, initially from Ireland but later from many other nations. However, it was often a very isolated presence, deeply unconnected to the activities of other Christian denominations and also to other social institutions in the very neighbourhoods in which these parish churches existed. Catholic schools and social clubs kept the Catholic population separated to some degree from the rest of the inner-city population.

The third phase described by Ward, possibly beginning as early as the 1920s, saw a shift in industrial production away from the city centre. That shift changed the landscape of the old urban cores to include government offices, financial institutions and corporate headquarters. After the Second World War, slum clearances in the inner city caused a further disruption of older working-class communities, with the creation in some cases of large estates built on the edge of cities, not part of the urban centre, but clearly distinct from middle-class suburbia. These estates, in the latter part of the twentieth century, are also sometimes included in the description of urban priority areas, even though in a geographical sense they are not actually in an urban setting.

It is during this phase that the alienation between the working classes and the Church becomes dramatically clear. In general we can talk of the flight of the Church from the inner city, sometimes characterized as 'white flight'. But although this is an accurate description of the overall picture, the reality on the ground is much more variegated and certainly differs in the particular stories of non-conformists, Anglicans and Roman Catholics.

A story of displacement

I am going to illustrate some of these differences by telling the story of one particular inner-city area. I am not suggesting that all inner-city areas are the same as this one, but it does illustrate, if not document, the lived experiences of many Christians in the inner city.

The neighbourhood in question was built in the latter part of the nineteenth century to provide accommodation for the working classes who provided labour for the surrounding areas. The housing was of low quality (sometimes called 'back to back') and the people were unquestionably poor. During the late nineteenth century up until 1945, the area was served by a number of churches: five non-conformist chapels, two Anglican parish churches, and one Catholic parish church.

After the Second World War, the city council took a decision to completely clear all the housing in this neighbourhood, since it was deemed to be unfit for human habitation, and virtually every building, including most of the churches, were to be demolished and then rebuilt, as part of the redevelopment plan. The Anglican and Catholic buildings, together with a few other public buildings, were the only structures not to be demolished.

Inevitably, this radical development, which took 20 years to complete, had a highly disruptive impact on the whole neighbourhood, and certainly on the life of the churches. The experience of the non-conformist churches, the Anglicans and the Catholics was rather different during this period. The development described above took place in stages and so the whole population was not moved simultaneously and, because of the staged nature of the project, it was possible for those who wished to move back once a certain stage had been completed to do so.

From the information that I was able to glean from conversations with the clergy and leading lay people during the 1970s, no single member of any of their congregations chose to return to the neighbourhood in question once the development had been completed and the church buildings had been rebuilt. The reasons for this were complex. In part, they were now familiar with the new homes and neighbourhoods in which they lived. The housing that had taken the place of their former homes often consisted of high-rise apartments and was not the kind to which they wished to return. Their web of relationships of family and friends no longer existed there. There were few obvious incentives to return.

What became clear is that the sense of place experienced by these congregations prior to the Second World War consisted of the complex communities woven together by bonds of family, long-term friendships, shared experiences and commitments, social events, church and Sunday school anniversaries. The church provided a home outside the immediate environment of the family home. Amid the hardships of life in the 1930s, here were places of safety, mutual support, encouragement and, to use a slightly older word, fellowship. This had been an important expression of community, and indeed pride in what working-class people could accomplish together. That sense of community was widened by the personal relationships that existed between the members of the various churches.

But however valuable these communities might be, they were also vulnerable. Although the Sunday congregations almost filled the available seats, among the non-conformist churches these were not large buildings. They could celebrate their work among youth and children, with large numbers of children regularly attending Sunday school, but in reality the membership often consisted of a relatively small number of large extended families. It did not take too much to disrupt these kinds of generational patterns, and the combination of war and redevelopment delivered disruption on a huge scale. It was difficult to find any children of those who joined these churches in the 1930s in attendance in the 1960s. These children, even if they had retained their faith, had grown up, had their own families, and had no intention of returning.

This did not mean that these churches had no congregations; they certainly did, but they consisted of the core of members, who elected to commute from their new homes located several miles from the church building. The demolition of housing had a decisive impact on the relationship between what had been very locally based congregations and the churches that they were still committed to attend.

But in reality the forced removal only exacerbated a trend that had been developing. The more successful members in terms of social mobility had been moving out of the neighbourhood for some time before the redevelopment took place.

Nevertheless, it left those congregations with a dramatically different relationship between the neighbourhood and the churches. For the most part, for several decades after the redevelopment had been completed, no one in these congregations actually lived in the neighbourhood and no one in the neighbourhood was part of these congregations. There was a slight feeling of a siege mentality, illustrated by the large car parks adjacent to the buildings, surrounded by high fences. These car parks were only used on a few occasions in the week – usually twice on Sundays and then on the occasional mid-week evenings when a meeting was due to take place. The filling and then emptying of the car parks were the only signs of life as far as the neighbourhood was concerned.

This was not just a matter of physical distance caused by the commuting phenomenon, but there was a difference too of values, habits, interests, aspirations, income and the ordinary aspects of daily living that made conversation less possible and comfortable. The question that every congregation was asking following the building of their churches was simply this, 'How do we re-plant our churches into this community, which was once part of our lives, from where we originally came, but which is now very unfamiliar to us?'

Each congregation took a different approach in attempting to answer that question, and to date, more than half a century after they entered their new buildings with hope in their hearts for a new beginning, few answers are forthcoming for the various non-conformist congregations. Some have closed and others continue to have a somewhat precarious existence.

The situation for the two Anglican parishes has been slightly different. The two parishes became one parish. The presence of an Anglican primary school and the ability to draw on resources from the diocese to pay clergy, re-order buildings and invest in community projects has slightly strengthened the congregation, but creating presence in the neighbourhood remains a struggle.

By contrast, the Roman Catholic parish became two parishes in the 1960s as part of the rebuilding programme and, although both parishes have faced some challenges, the presence of a Catholic primary school, and other social institutions, has helped to connect these congregations to their immediate community. Immigration from Ireland, but increasingly from other nations, has meant that the Catholic community has remained fairly significant in this inner-city area.

The Sunday attendance at the two Catholic churches is significantly higher than the combined Sunday attendance of all the Protestant churches. In that sense, the Catholic Church represents the single most effective Christian presence in this neighbourhood. However, it is debatable whether that presence ever reaches beyond the already existing numbers of people who identified themselves as Catholics prior to their arrival in this inner-city area, as a result of the activity of the Catholic Church in other countries. Maintenance rather than mission seems to have been the dominant theme over the last 50 years for the Catholic Church.

But that does not mean that nothing has changed in the relationship between the churches and their locale in the neighbourhood we are describing. Three significant changes have taken place in the past 40 years. First is the arrival of two new Christian congregations. Both are predominantly West Indian. Their members live partly in the immediate community but are also drawn from a much wider geographic area. Commitment to the denomination and to the very specific forms of West Indian cultural life is a dominating theme. It is unlikely that many local people who are not themselves West Indians would consider joining these congregations.

A second change is the arrival of African Christians in the immediate neighbourhood over the past 20 years. Interestingly, for the most part these Christians have chosen to join local white -majority congregations rather than begin new congregations. Undoubtedly, some African Christians commute out of the area to attend African-led churches, although this is difficult to document. In some cases the trend to join local white-majority churches has been sufficiently strong that these congregations may in time become black-majority congregations, although, at the moment, leadership remains largely white. That trend has benefited all expressions of church life in the neighbourhood, except ironically the two West Indian-majority congregations.

The third development is the arrival of significant numbers of Muslims from a wide variety of nations. Their presence represents a challenge to the churches and there seems to be little communication between these two world faiths.

These changes contribute to a fracturing of the community, a loss of cohesion and a subsequent erosion of any sense of place, of history and of identity. This is often a place where people do not stay long – it is a transitory place. To some extent, the massive disruption in this area can be traced back to the decision of the city council to demolish the existing housing and to replace it with forms of housing that have not been helpful in re-creating community.

The churches have attempted to form worshipping communities and from these locales to bring some help and hope to a very needy area of the city. But it has undoubtedly been a struggle, partly because the various Protestant Christian Churches are not deeply located in the community but rely on personnel from outside the neighbourhood, partly because the small size of these congregations leaves them with few resources and tends to focus attention on survival rather than service, and partly because it is not clear what mission looks like in this area beyond occasional attempts at the evangelization of individuals.

Even though this story is given a particular edge because of the redevelopment of the physical landscape, the themes of impermanence, disruption, mobility and the difficulty for anyone living in the inner city of developing roots in that locale still seem to permeate many stories from such areas. Partly this is about power, and specifically the lack of power to influence what happens in the immediate locale. It feels as though things are done *to* people in the name of doing things *for* people.

A story of remaining

In contrast to the previous story, I want to offer a very different experience. I am not suggesting that this story is in any way normative – indeed, the very fact that it is not normative is part of its importance. It is a story of stability within the context of a profoundly changing community. The community in question is also one that has experienced profound change as the predominantly white working-class population has moved out and other communities have moved in. The change has happened over a period of 40 years, and very rapidly over the past 20 years.

These changes have resulted in some interesting complexity, where no single community dominates. Approximately one-third of the people originate from the Indian subcontinent, close to 30 per cent describe themselves as white (British or Irish or another), while around 12 per cent identify as black Africans. The remainder come from a huge number of backgrounds, with most nations on earth represented.

This diversity is reflected in religious affiliation. Some 40 per cent identify as Christian, 32 per cent as Muslim, nearly 10 per cent as Hindu, with a sizeable Sikh population constituting 2 per cent of the population. Nearly 10 per cent indicate that they have no religious affiliation, which is somewhat lower than other parts of the country. The rapidity of the changes in the make-up of the population contributes to the sense that this is a community that has lost touch with its roots, its history and its sense of identity. Many of the newly arrived derive their identity from the nations and culture from which they have recently come. In addition to this complexity, around 25 per cent of households do not have English as the main language in their home.

Amid this swirling drama of change, there lies a fascinating story of remaining. One particular family, part of a local non-conformist church, has made a conscious decision to remain amid the change, not just for one or two generations but for five generations. The point of this story is not so much the commitment of a remarkable family to a particular neighbourhood as what this decision has engendered.

The church moved from its own building (which it has also retained) to rejuvenate a local community centre that now effectively operates as the main base for the worshipping congregation. Many community initiatives have emanated from this building, including sports activities.

These activities have forged a new relationship with a much-changed community at the same time as rebuilding connections with many in the white working-class community who did not move out. Many different nationalities have joined this growing church. In addition, the church has been able to facilitate worship space for other congregations who worship in different languages and with very different worship styles.

The combination of this careful and sensitive building of relationships with many groups within the community has gradually built what we might describe as a growing 'new culture'. The new culture is able to celebrate both the differences that are contained within the surrounding streets and the history of all that has taken place in this neighbourhood over many years. By consciously making connections between the past and embracing a very different present, something very creative is beginning to take place.

Part of the explanation for this development lies in the collective memory of the five generations of the family who remained. The present generation within this family have had educational opportunities, and professional occupations that normally would have resulted in a move to other, more prosperous areas. The decision to remain is seen within the context of a particular understanding of their Christian faith. That is not to say that Christians are not also sent to other places to pursue mission, but sometimes mission means remaining and creating the charism of stability – so important in times of rapid change.

These contrasting stories help to illustrate that inner-city contexts, while sharing some characteristics, all have their own unique and distinctive histories, stories and features. It would be possible to keep telling unique stories from the inner city, but what these stories all highlight (stories told and untold) is that the inner-city experience is not static; it is constantly changing.

A number of mission organizations have made it their core purpose to begin new congregations in the inner city, often encouraging gifted leaders to move into areas of deprivation. That is a costly commitment and it flows from the conviction that mission cannot be conducted on the basis of commuting – it has to take context and place seriously, sufficiently seriously that where one lives is as important as the programmes that one might initiate. In that sense, the commitment of the Anglican Church in particular to maintain a widespread presence in the inner city is laudable, albeit often difficult.

Many inner-city contexts contain stories of new opportunities, partly because new cultures keep arriving, but also because inner-city settings are often places of great creativity and opportunity. There is an important sense in which our inner cities are places that help to shape and develop the wider culture. This is partly through regeneration initiatives, partly through the arts, but also because faith – not just the Christian faith – is seen as a resource that continues to bring human dignity and hope.

What we are seeing therefore, beyond the initial phenomenon of 'white flight', is an attempt to re-engage with the context of the inner city, not simply from the previous, largely pastoral perspective, but more with a missional intent. That gives a different feel to the approaches that are taken and almost certainly attracts a wider variety of ministry giftings. There seems to be a recognition among many who are accepting a call to this kind of ministry that they do not engage as experts but as learners, listening first to what God might be doing in a given context.

In the midst of these many experiments, many surprises

emerge. One Anglican 'pioneer minister' told me of the surprise he encountered towards the end of his first year of ministry. He had come to a deprived urban priority area with a largely white working-class parish. The small group of worshippers (around 30) had grown somewhat through the introduction of a small ministry team who had created a number of community activities. The worshipping community had grown to about 70 people. To his astonishment, around 600 people turned up for worship at the main Christmas celebration. These are the people described by the sociologist Grace Davie as 'believing but not belonging', but notions of belonging in this working-class parish were perhaps stronger than the pioneering team had imagined. The church might be perceived as remote from everyday life, and regular religious practice might be weak, but the sense that this was still their parish church, an important connection in the place where they lived, was given a visceral expression in this annual Christmas attendance.

We could characterize most of the mission initiatives in relation to inner-city neighbourhoods as either church planting, re-planting or revitalization. Although these are certainly distinct approaches, especially concerning leadership and resources, the basic underlying ministry principles and actions are not actually very different across these categories. There are at least three key questions that emerge for missional pioneers in these settings.

First, who now lives here and, second, who now feels a sense of belonging here? It is very clear that some who have come to live in inner-city areas see their location as a permanent home. This is where they now live and where they expect to see their children and grandchildren living. They are not anticipating a move in the foreseeable future.

The Christian community has an important role in helping to create some stability in the midst of rapid change, whether that change relates to population shift or to economic deprivation caused by the decline of the traditional industries that previously gave sustenance and identity to some inner-city areas.

The question about who lives here now is at its sharpest in relation to the very large concentration of Muslims, particularly those from the Indian subcontinent who have formed very distinct communities, sometimes comprised of those who came from the same rural village and who now live in the same street. Rural Pakistan, Bangladesh or parts of northern India can be re-created in community terms in the streets of Birmingham, Burnley or Bradford. That leads to the third missional question: 'How does Christian mission see its role in relation to these communities of Muslims, and also of Hindus and Sikhs?'

What sense of permanence do those who are living in the neighbourhood have? There are some for whom life in inner- city Britain is a very temporary staging point; they desire to move as soon as possible, to a different part of the city, to another city or even, in some cases, back to the country in which they were born. What does Christian mission look like for these people? Is it to provide a place of temporary welcome and community while their lives are reorientated, or is it to make it possible for such people to take a different stance in relation to their 'temporary' surroundings and to begin to see that God might have a purpose and a calling for them in their new home?

What is the Christian community attempting to accomplish? Does the Church simply look for converts and sufficient new members to enable it to be sustainable? Or is the strength of the Christian community actually related to a deeper commitment to these neighbourhoods? Especially in those many places that have experienced large-scale immigration, is it possible that the Church might become the catalyst for a new kind of culture, an emerging sense of what it might mean to be British because one is a Christian first and foremost? Intercultural churches rather than multicultural churches could be locales of rich discovery– not so much of a promised land, but a land where promises are made, deep promises that help to form the commitments that create stable communities.

I remember taking part in a worship service in a congregation of largely Zimbabwean people, where the pastor led a kind of benedictory song that named the city in which they were meeting and declared, 'This is our territory, this is our land!' This commitment to place was significant and very moving.

Notes

1 Graham Ward, *Cities of God* (Abingdon: Routledge, 2000), pp. 32f.

2 Ward, *Cities*, pp. 34ff.

3 The Report of the Archbishop of Canterbury's Commission on Urban Priority Areas, *Faith in the City: A Call for Action by Church and Nation* (London: Church House Publishing, 1985), p. 28.

4 Archbishop of Canterbury, *Faith*, p. 28.

5 Archbishop of Canterbury, *Faith*, p. 28.

6 Archbishop of Canterbury, *Faith*, p. 28.

5

Fresh Expressions as a Manifestation of Particular Place

Simply doing better what one has always done may not be enough. Fresh eyes, fresh leadership, and so a fresh expression of mission and Christian community, may be needed to allow the Christian community to break out of existing patterns of life that may be driven by a small number of people – even, perhaps, dominated by cliques.

The immediate sequence of events that gave rise to the Fresh Expressions initiative within the Church of England is fairly straightforward to document and understand. Fresh Expressions as an organization came into being fairly soon after the former Archbishop of Canterbury, Rowan Williams, took up his post in 2003. The initiative did not simply arise from nowhere. There were a number of developments in the Anglican Church that together have helped to shape the thinking that led to the creation of Fresh Expressions.

The Fresh Expressions website contains a section on the Fresh Expressions story that includes these words:

> In the late 1990s and into the New Millennium, a number of Church denominations and mission agencies worked together reflecting on the 90s church-planting movement and beginning a process of investing and encouraging the pioneering of new forms of church expression. These fresh expressions weren't simply a fad or an attempt to be cool but

looked to address a rapidly changing culture in the UK and a change in attitude to attending church and to a spiritual life. New things were taking place and church expressions like The Net in Huddersfield and Grace in Ealing sought to re-imagine church for this new environment whilst staying true to a missional and Christ-centred gospel.[1]

The reference to the '90s church-planting movement' is an important one and requires some further explanation. To a certain extent, that movement had some important origins with an Anglican initiative in St Helen's led by Bob and Mary Hopkins in a partnership with YWAM. That initiative, together with some other developments among the Baptists with their Frontline teams and the Methodists and their Seed teams, signalled that there was a difference between church extension and church planting.

Church extension in new housing areas had always taken place and essentially consisted of the provision of a building, a clergyperson (or team) and a programme, essentially for those Christians who could be expected to move to a new area. Of course, evangelism was certainly on the agenda of such new starts, but it was just one of the many issues that a church operating in an essentially Christendom mindset would develop. Different kinds of churchmanship would have a variety of approaches to the evangelistic task.

The kind of church planting being undertaken by the Hopkins team, and by some of the other teams mentioned above, operated on a different basis. These teams put mission at the heart of their activity – not providing services of one kind or another for existing Christians. That gave them – in fact necessitated their developing – new kinds of flexibility with regard to staffing. New buildings were not on the agenda.

Recognizing this shift in tone and culture, a number of senior church leaders invited the Bible Society in England and Wales to host a consultation on church planting. That consultation

THE PLACE OF THE PARISH

was held at the High Leigh Conference Centre in 1990. Around 40 leaders from most of the major denominations, and many of the smaller denominations, attended by invitation only. YWAM led by Lynn Green, the Pioneer network led by Gerald Coates and the Ichthus Fellowship led by Roger and Faith Foster were highly involved in the organization of this event. This was partly because Lynn Green had been impressed by what he had seen of the DAWN church planting movement. DAWN had originated in the Philippines and had subsequently expanded its core ideas and principles to a number of nations around the world. It was essentially a saturation church-planting movement.

Lynn Green, together with Roger Foster and Gerald Coates, suggested adopting this methodology in the UK under the banner of Challenge 2000. The concept was to attempt to plant 20,000 churches by the year 2000. Part of the methodology was to hold a number of Congresses at which goals for church planting would be adopted by the participating denominations and then progress assessed at subsequent events.

The first Congress was held in Birmingham in 1992. At this event the Anglican representatives suggested that they would attempt 10,000 church plants by the year 2000. The problem with this approach was at least twofold. First, few if any of the denominations that adopted goals had any infrastructure to enable planting on this scale to take place. Second, there was little thought given to what church planting would actually look like. For the most part, the planting that was attempted was to create more congregations that used a model of church that represented a fairly traditional approach to planting. In other words, planting meant more of the same, not more of something radically different.

Somewhat inevitably, the Challenge 2000 movement came to an end before the close of the decade in which this was all being attempted. At a superficial level, this all looked like failure and the immediate result was that church planting came off the agenda of most denominations. The exception was the activity of black-majority churches, mostly based within the African diaspora living in the UK, which were planting churches fairly vigorously, but not within the framework of Challenge 2000.

To a certain extent this was the transplanting of the vigorous life of African Christianity to Western countries. These were also traditional attempts at church planting, although the intention was often to plant churches from an African base and then to reach out to the white-majority host community. In reality, very few of these churches succeeded in their desire to reach beyond the ethnic group with which they began.

Despite taking church planting off the agenda, the white-majority churches began to ask a series of questions in the light of their failure to church plant on any scale. The most important of these was the fundamental question, 'What do we mean by church?' and so, by extension, 'What do we mean by church planting?'

Within Anglican circles, in the 1990s, a study examined the issue of the effectiveness of parish churches in relation to the size of a parish. The conclusion, not surprisingly, was that the percentage of people attending the parish church fell dramatically once parishes became larger than 5,000 people. More significantly, it was also clear that where parishes contained a number of socioeconomic groups, the parish church tended to reach only those sections of the parish that were understood to be property-owning middle-class people. Clearly, if parish churches were really to serve the whole of a parish, something different needed to happen to reach those parts of the parish that were largely untouched by the local parish church.

Moreover, there were many occasions when, even within the orbit of the middle classes, parish churches were not very effective in reaching those who had traditionally not seen themselves as churchgoers. There was a sense that in some parishes, possibly even the majority of parishes, a culture had developed that was not open to those who were perceived as 'outsiders'. This was not a deliberate attempt to keep others out so much as a failure to understand the extent to which the culture had taken a different direction from that of the church. There was a gulf of understanding or even misunderstanding. Those who had been nurtured within the life of the Church found it hard to appreciate the extent to which those outside the Church found church culture baffling, strange and irrelevant.

As the Anglican Church moved beyond the issue of the nature of church and hence the potential shape of church planting, they also moved into a new decade and a new century with a new Archbishop of Canterbury. A key appointment in the Church of England was that of Graham Cray as Bishop of Maidstone. The intention of this appointment was that he would assist the Archbishop of Canterbury with thinking around evangelism and mission. As part of this task a study was commissioned, *Mission-Shaped Church*, which reflected some of the earlier work of the Springboard team and that of Robert Warren, all of which had run in parallel with the Challenge 2000 initiative. Springboard was the Initiative for Evangelism of the Archbishops of Canterbury and York. Robert Warren also wrote a helpful book, *Building Missionary Congregations*, which could be seen as a contributory building block in terms of the *Mission-Shaped Church* publication.

However, the *Mission-Shaped Church* study went beyond that earlier thinking and fed into a report from a working group of the Mission and Public Affairs Council of the Church of England. This group was chaired by Graham Cray and presented a major report in the April of 2004. The report contained these words:

> The reality of church planting has been not of quantity but diversity. Common themes within that diversity:
>
> - Church derives its self-understanding from the mission of God's love to the world. Trinity models diversity as well as unity.
> - Creation reveals diversity.

- Mission to a diverse world legitimately requires a diverse Church.
- Catholicity is not monochrome oneness.
- God is culturally specific within diverse contexts.

The planting process is the engagement of church and gospel with a new mission context, and this should determine fresh expression of church.[2]

This report led directly to the creation of the Fresh Expressions initiative, which began its work in September 2004 under the leadership of Steven Croft. One of the early tasks of Fresh Expressions was to work to change legislation within the Church of England such that the 'mixed economy' might have room to flourish. One of the most significant developments was the creation of Bishops' Mission Orders (BMOs), which was designed to break the veto of a parish priest over missional experiments in their particular parish. Alongside this new order, the Anglican Church has sought to create a new kind of ministry, Pioneer Ministry, which was and is designed to bring into ministry a parallel ministry stream that allows individuals to function in experimental forms of church. In addition, the Anglicans brought the Methodist Church into the Fresh Expressions partnership at an early stage.

Facing the critics

As one might expect with a major new initiative, there was push-back of various kinds. Some of the criticism realized that the legislative changes represented a rather decisive shift in the way in which the Church of England acted, or prevented action. But the combination of good leadership, support from the hierarchy, adequate if not lavish financial support, and a shift on the ground towards the more evangelical and charismatic wing of the Church meant that this kind of opposition was not very effective. Moreover, the leadership of Fresh Expressions gave space for the Anglo-Catholic wing of the Church to make their distinctive contribution. The strong support from within Fresh Expressions for 'inherited modes' of the Church as valid, welcomed and wanted also helped to create a genuine sense that there was a commitment to a mixed economy as compared to the advocacy of the latest fad.

A second kind of push-back was more a theological critique, and that kind of critique was not dismissed by the Fresh Expressions team, but engaged with. The substance of the theological issues were raised in the publication *Mission-shaped Church: A Theological Response*, by John Hull, and *Mission-shaped Questions: Defining Issues for Today's Church*, authored from within the Fresh Expressions team. A later book, *Testing Fresh Expressions: Identity and Transformation*, by John Walker, attempted a detailed analysis of the claims of Fresh Expressions at the grass-roots level. These were not hostile questions or defensive responses in tone, but they were questions that were interrogative in nature, partly seeking more understanding of the issues raised by Fresh Expressions, and partly expressing some reserve.

A third kind of more practical critique came from those who had attempted a Fresh Expression and found that it had not gone so well. A very touching and thoughtful article was published in the *Church Times*,[3] written by a clergy person who had led a Fresh Expression of church that had subsequently closed. He made six helpful observations in the article, all of which are intended to be helpful, but most of which also reveal a level of pain that is experienced by those who engage in such an exercise but who find that it does not go according to plan. His key observation is probably his first point, in which he speaks of the management of expectations.

Some 20 years on

Nearly 20 years after the thinking around Fresh Expressions began, a number of features have become clear. First, the nature of Fresh Expressions is to be experimental. On one level that allows for creativity and it also tends to bring into ministry those who would not be attracted to the traditional priesthood. But experimentation also means a degree of learning from the experience. Not every experiment will succeed and, if expectations are well managed, that does not have to lead to a feeling of failure so much as a reflection on lessons learnt and carried into the next attempt at a Fresh Expression of church.

Second, the diversity that was alluded to in a quote earlier in this chapter is very evident, almost bewilderingly so. That can lead to a degree of cynicism, captured in the comment of one minister who recognized that his local version of a Fresh Expression had pre-dated the Fresh Expressions report, but who candidly acknowledged that he had just rebranded his mission effort as a Fresh Expression because that brought funding. However, even that reaction is not necessarily a bad thing as the Church learns to work with a radically different situation – a mission field and not a pastoral field.

Third, the sheer number of experiments – apart from the diversity – is astonishing. Research commissioned by Fresh Expressions between 2012 and 2016 identified 1,109 Fresh Expressions of church in 21 of the 43 dioceses, with 50,600 attending these worshipping communities. That is around 5 per cent of the total number of Anglican worshippers. Some of these Fresh Expressions also identify themselves as 'Messy Church', which does add a layer of complexity to keeping track of what is taking place. Messy Church is not an Anglican initiative per se. It is a ministry that operates under the umbrella of the Bible Reading Fellowship with 2,800 registered groups in the UK and 3,500 worldwide.

Within the Anglican Community there is a huge degree of ambition in terms of using Fresh Expressions as a mission tool.

The diocese of Leicester, which has 234 parishes and 324 church buildings within those parishes, has spoken of an ambition to have a Fresh Expression of church in every parish. The recently appointed chair of Fresh Expressions, Bishop Ric Thorpe, has spoken of a vision to see at least 10,000 Fresh Expressions of church in the Anglican Church. This is strangely reminiscent of the earlier commitment to plant 10,000 churches in relation to the Challenge 2000 movement, but this time the ambition is supported by recruitment, training, funding and an infrastructure that makes these kinds of goals a possibility.

So is Fresh Expressions a form of church planting or is church planting a form of Fresh Expressions? At one level the answer to this question doesn't really matter. There are situations where both could be true. But at another level there is a question that needs to be explored. Graham Cray gives four descriptors of a Fresh Expression as follows:

- Missional – serving people outside church.
- Contextual – listening to people and entering their culture.
- Educational – making discipleship a priority.
- Ecclesial – forming church.

We could certainly debate the description of missional as 'serving people outside church', but more important in this debate is the issue of context. Fresh Expressions has a concern to allow the context to shape the Church. In other words, mission is primary and the Church is what happens when disciples are formed in a context. My own view is that this is a very helpful approach to both a theology and also a practice of mission, not just in the context of the West but in any context.

However, it opens a debate about the relationship of context to place. Fresh Expressions is primarily concerned to reach those who the parish church is failing to meet, those who are outside the orbit of the Church. That means focusing on groups before thinking about geography, which can mean place but not necessarily so.

The following extract, written by me, was originally published in the *Journal of Missional Practice*. It highlights a ministry that is focused on a people group located well outside the Church. The person leading the ministry does not regard this as a Fresh Expression of church as such, and yet the approach, although at one end of the spectrum, focusing on interest groups rather than geographic place, is illustrative of a number of experiments in the Fresh Expressions quiver:

Many people in the Western world do not experience place as a significant factor in their lives. Their relationships matter, as do their choices and self-expression, their particular stand among the cultures of late modernity. They seek out people who are like them and connect to networks which agree with their choices and these may extend over a wide geographical area. If they are aware of place as a factor, they may feel it to be a constraint which limits their options for change and growth.

Andrea Campanale lives in Kingston-upon-Thames, a region close to London where she was an elder in a charismatic church, wondering about her ministry. Her connections with people outside the church were important and she felt she had failed a friend who had had an unexpected spiritual experience, an audible voice speaking reassurance at a fearful moment. She had found it difficult to find the language to help her friend, and connect the experience with the gospel. But newly sensitive to spiritual seekers in our culture, she began to attend Kingston Green Fair and other creative events and look for opportunities to speak about faith and pray with people. Andrea and other Kingston Christians set up 'Sacred Space' in the town, and organized artistic events which had the potential to open up questions of faith. She learned a listening and prophetic prayer practice, a form of 'card reading', Ruach Cards,[4] which made a way into faith conversations.

Andrea used the language of 'space' (Sacred Space) to describe the opportunities they created for talk and listening and, she felt, divine encounter. This seemed to be a kind of protected space which allowed the possibility of an encounter with God despite distrust and misconceptions about Christianity. They made space for an experience of God which could not be controlled, which felt protected from human agency or manipulation.

Andrea was meeting many people at an early stage of their journey towards Christ, and many of these encounters were fleeting. New Christians were fragile. She attempted to put some seekers into connection with more mature Christians from the church, but this initiative faltered partly through a lack of confidence among the Christians. Eventually she set up the group she now describes as a missional community. She doesn't describe this as a form of church, or even a 'fresh expression'. It is a community; they share in each other's lives. But as the leader her role is to help members of her community discern their vocation and find the confidence to enter into mission in their contexts, in the place where they are. A newly retired woman wanted to serve as a chaplain in her own town centre. Andrea provided the entrepreneurial skill to get her started.

This form of leadership has connected Andrea with a few striking sub-cultures. One member of the missional community is part of the Steam Punk network, a group which takes a stand against current styles, in their elaborate Victorian clothing and in their love of complicated pre-electronic technology. Andrea hasn't tried to enter this network herself, or draw people from it into Sacred Space. She does participate in events with her friend, acting as a mentor and supporting and helping him to find opportunities to talk about faith and nurture a group in that context. She does take her Ruach Cards along.

Listening to Andrea one had the impression that the

Sacred Space events and ministries, perhaps especially the card reading, communicates the expectation that God does speak and God acts. Why is the concept of space important and what does this bring that is different to place? For some people on occasion, and especially in an oppressively secular culture, is it helpful to step away from the limitations, the 'rebarbative' particularities of place, and enter a space which makes more room for imagination?[5]

While it is true that most Fresh Expressions of church do operate within the consciousness of a parish, and hence a place, it is not necessarily the case that those who connect with these experiments see the proposition around place as being as significant as community. One can argue that it is difficult to explore or develop community without reference to a place and its particularities. But it is also likely that relationships and their visceral reality come before an awareness of their location in a particular place.

To return to Graham Cray's four descriptors of Fresh Expressions, he emphasizes discipleship as his third point and the formation of church as his fourth point. Some might find the emphasis on discipleship surprising, partly because some want to push for conversion with little thought given to discipleship, and partly because the creation of disciples as compared with believers is a difficult thing to do. Yet, strangely, difficult as it might be, it is also contextually creative. Ann Morisy, writing in her book that is subtitled *Community Ministry and Mission,* says this:

In a society such as ours where scepticism is the norm, it may be more appropriate to begin by promoting discipleship rather than belief. Through the expression of discipleship, especially discipleship which speaks of venturesome love, it is likely that people will encounter experiences that are relevant to their half-formed faith; more than this, some of the great themes of the Gospel can come alive. When people express the venturesome love, which is at the heart of Christian discipleship, they also begin a process of discerning God's involvement in the world. Community ministry harnesses this dynamic by means of – group discussion as part of the support for volunteers involved in the venture; formal and informal spiritual direction provided by an appropriately skilled pastor; the introduction of occasional (apt liturgy) into the life of the venture.

This process presents two major challenges to local churches. The first is to develop the skills to enable such a process to take place. The second is more profound and requires the local church to understand its missionary task as that of encouraging people to do business with God and to contribute to God's purposes for humankind. This is quite different from encouraging people to come to Church and worship Sunday by Sunday.[6]

Community ministry by its very nature deals with complex personal relationships situated in a context or place. Participation is always in connection with a community of people formed around the kind of everyday activities that nevertheless raise existential questions. Arguably, that kind of web of relationships often provides a safe space in which existential questions can be explored. Ann Morisy again:

The chief reason, in terms of mission, for inviting participation is that through it people will become open to experiences which resonate with their often unspoken awareness of issues of 'ultimate concern'. Through their commitment to a struggle which is wider than their own well-being, people are enabled to muse on the big questions of life. Does my life and the lives of those with whom I am involved have any meaning? Does the world in which I am cast without my consent have any purpose? This urge to engage with such metaphysical issues is also part of our humanity …

For the most part, encounter with God and the bursting out of the new creation occur not in some special spiritual time or zone but through and amid the vicissitudes, conflicts and contingency of our everyday life.[7]

Luke Bretherton, writing from a rather different set of experiences, nevertheless shares with Ann Morisy a conviction that it is the ordinary – or even the mundane – that creates the framework for discipleship to be generated:

In emphasising the mundane and the ordinary as the primary area of our transforming encounter with God I am not denigrating the importance of the ecstatic and euphoric intensity of God's presence that can be experienced in worship. I am seeking to locate such intense moments of corporate and personal encounter with God in their proper place. Such moments are only part (albeit a vital part) of the rhythm of the Christian life that, as the liturgical year teaches us, has three basic modes …

The third mode of the Christian life is ordinary time … It is this ordinary time that is, perhaps, the focus of a mundane holiness and it is ordinary time that is, perhaps, the major key or predominant mode of the Christian life. Those, like Peter, who followed Jesus, experienced times of feasting and intimacy as well as times of trial and suffering, but for the most part, life with Jesus, and the transformation of their life this involved, took place within the everyday and mundane context of their relationships with each other, with their families, and how they lived the practicalities of life within the prevailing social, economic and political realities of the day. To refuse to live faithfully in ordinary time and constantly seek times of ecstasy (as some mystic, ritualistic, charismatic and Pentecostal Christians do) or insist that all of life is a fast (as some over-ascetic and legalistic Christians do) is to refuse, as I have argued above, a definitive part of Christian discipleship.[8]

These grounded sets of relationships take time to develop, and that produces another tension for those engaged in primary mission in pioneering situations. Because it takes a long time to produce healthy communities, this can clash with the expectation of those who are overseeing and funding experiments of this kind and who are often hoping for discernible progress – if not a quick fix. How to bridge the gap between initial funding and the eventual development of a worshipping community based on discipleship will remain a practical consideration.

One pioneer, deeply grounded in a church that has developed a long-term relationship with its immediate community, wrote a book about these experiences, with the telling title *Slow Church*. He writes:

> The Sunday night conversation has been a means of grace to me. It has taught me to slow down. I'm learning to be more attentive to the people around me, and to the specific opportunities posed by our neighborhood. When I came to Englewood, I was an activist at heart. I wanted to speed through conversations, make decisions and get things done now, regardless of the collateral damage. I have seen enough over the years to know that God is at work in our midst and that things do get done, though maybe not on my timetable. I am learning to be content with slow progress.[9]

In the case of this particular church in the United States, it took from the 1960s, when 'white flight' from the inner city began, to the second decade of the twenty-first century for them to finally figure out what God might be creating in this community context. Half a century is a long time to wait for results!

Church-shaped mission or mission-shaped church?

Inevitably, the creation of Fresh Expressions of church raises a number of questions about the nature of mission. The first question is whether the very emphasis on church causes missiology to tend to collapse into ecclesiology, which was part of John Hull's critique in *Mission-shaped Church*, meaning that the initiative could lean towards church-shaped mission rather than mission-shaped church:

> Where then does mission-shaped thinking about the church, properly begin? It begins with God, with theology, reflection upon and talk about God. Just as we cannot look at our own eyes without a mirror for reflection, so the church is unable to see itself for what it is without seeing itself via something else. Mission-shaped thinking suggests that the 'something else' is the God of mission.[10]

The second question that is raised concerns the relationship between the Church and the kingdom of God. This question is directly explored in a chapter by John Hull in *Mission-shaped Questions*, under the heading, 'Mission-shaped and Kingdom Focused?' Hull's claim is that missiology requires a focus on the kingdom, not just the Church.

A third question that also flows from a discussion on the nature of the kingdom of God relates to the way in which mission-shaped church connects to very specific questions about the witness of the Church to culture. Specifically, the issue of whether the Church should be involved in the transformation of culture, as compared with the idea – sometimes associated with evangelicals – that as you convert individuals, the culture necessarily changes.

Also in *Mission-shaped Questions*, the theologian Graham Tomlin explores the tension contained in seeking to engage a culture while simultaneously expressing the unique culture of the Church as a community that worships God and is a sign of the kingdom. The aim of the Church must be not only to understand the 'target' culture, but also to seek to transform the wider culture in which that target culture is located. He comments:

> Fresh expressions of church are well placed to do this kind of work, because they tend to be communities of Christians well attuned to the culture of their target audience. But if they are to transform the cultures which they are trying to reach, they will need to be as attentive, if not more so, to the question of how they express the culture of the kingdom as they are to the question of how they relate to their target culture. If they fail to ask this question, they will tend to blend into the culture so much that they will become indistinguishable. It then becomes hard to see the point in joining a community that is just a religious version of the surrounding culture. If, however, they can embody and cultivate the true culture of church, the life of the Spirit in a way that shows particular cultures exactly what they are missing, they can have an exciting future.[11]

The lure of 'successful' church

In the past decade there have been some hopeful and encouraging developments within the Anglican Church in terms of mission, although these have faced criticism from the more traditional wing of the Church. There has also been the tendency, not confined to Anglican churches, to brand an activity or programme as 'missional' merely to add some kudos to it or in the hope it will somehow breathe new life into past endeavours. In these cases churches are being tempted to use the idea of 'missional' with the aim of becoming more 'successful' as churches. It also draws attention from planting truly 'fresh expressions' of church to the hope of 'freshening up' existing expressions of church.

There is a danger therefore that, in the Anglican Church as well as in other churches, missional church or mission-shaped church becomes seen merely as a vehicle for creating or developing 'successful' churches, and that the realization of this will result in cynicism. The missional church conversation is one of the most hopeful movements to emerge in the last decade. This is partly why the term has so quickly come to acceptance and use throughout the Church today. It is an indication of the Church's own self-searching for ways to understand its current malaise. Yet the way in which the missional conversation is being taken up in some quarters may be one more sign of our own captivity to the long echo of our Christendom past. If the Church is only looking to find church answers to its questions about how to turn the tide of declining attendance and financial resources by becoming a better, bigger, more successful Church, then it will not be in dialogue with its culture but only trying to work out tactics and programmes that will attract more people into the Church.

In this event, Fresh Expressions will not produce missional churches or missional movements of the people of God but will remain trapped in the Christendom heritage where the preoccupation is still the Church. The need is to continue to hear Scripture and listen to the culture. Fresh Expressions and other such missional initiatives must escape the agenda of church success and church growth by keeping the focus on God's love and care for the particular contexts of their neighbourhoods and communities.

Notes

1 Fresh Expressions website, https://freshexpressions.org.uk/about/our-story/.
2 The Mission-shaped Church working group, *Mission-shaped Church: Church Planting and Fresh Expressions of Church in a Changing Context* (London: Church House Publishing, 2004), p. 20.

3 Richard Kellow, 'Questions for Fresh Expressions', *Church Times*, 11 May 2018, www.churchtimes.co.uk/articles/2018/11-may/comment/opinion/questions-for-fresh-expressions.

4 Ruach Cards, www.ruachcards.co.uk/.

5 Martin Robinson interviews Andrea Campanale, 'Sacred Space', *Journal of Missional Practice* 10 (Winter 2018), http://journalofmissionalpractice. com/?s=andrea.

6 Ann Morisy, *Beyond the Good Samaritan: Community Ministry and Mission* (London: Mowbray, 1997), pp. 42f.

7 Morisy, *Beyond*, p. 45f.

8 Luke Bretherton, 'Mundane Holiness: The Theology and Spirituality of Everyday Life', in Andrew Walker and Luke Bretherton (eds), *Remembering our Future: Explorations in Deep Church* (London: Paternoster, 2007), pp. 236f.

9 C. Christopher Smith and John Pattison, *Slow Church: Cultivating Community in the Patient Way of Jesus* (Downers Grove, IL: IVP, 2014), pp. 219f.

10 Martyn Atkins, *Changing Church for a Changing World: Fresh Ways of Being Church in a Methodist Context* (Methodist Church Communication Office, 2007), p. 23.

11 Graham Tomlin, 'Can We Develop Churches that can Transform the Culture?', in Steven Croft (ed.) *Mission-shaped Questions: Defining Issues for Today's Church* (London: Church House Publishing, 2008), p. 77.

6

The Challenge of the Rural

We need to be cautious about speaking of the rural scene as if it has a uniform culture simply because it is rural. There are clearly huge differences between fairly isolated rural situations in places such as mid-Wales, Cumbria, Cornwall and East Anglia as compared with places that are still rural, but that are located near large cities and towns. Government studies make that distinction by categorizing rural contexts as either having populations that are 'not sparse' or 'in a sparse setting'. Local authority categories use a slightly different set of categories: 'mainly rural, largely rural and urban with significant rural populations'.

In recent years there has been a slight growth in the rural population. This has been partly caused by the desire of those who have lived in urban areas to enjoy a more rural environment and partly because of the recent policy of the UK government of encouraging the significant expansion of villages by easing planning restrictions on new housing. In addition to the move of some to live permanently in a rural setting, there is also the phenomenon of second home ownership, which not only distorts the economic and social life of villages but tends to price local people out of the housing market.

The general growth in population in rural areas tends to reinforce an existing disparity in the population make-up. In general, the population in rural areas is older than that in urban areas, with the number of those in their late teens and early twenties being considerably lower in the rural setting than in urban contexts. Older teenagers and those in their twenties tend to move to urban areas for further study and to take advantage of different employment opportunities. Those who move at this age tend not to return and this represents a permanent loss of talent and skills to rural communities, quite apart from the disruption caused to family and social frameworks.

The relative exodus of younger people from rural areas is mirrored by the gradual erosion of amenities such as shops, banks, pubs, post offices, doctor's surgeries, public transport and schools. Non-conformist churches have struggled to maintain a presence in many rural areas whereas the Anglican Church has mostly kept a parish system alive, even if clergy have had to serve an ever-increasing number of churches in the parish. Of all the institutions in many villages, the parish church is often the very last to close and can sometimes host other amenities such as shops, banks and post offices.

Underlying many of the challenges that face rural communities is the issue of mobility that we described in Chapter 1. The combination of the car and the internet enables those in rural areas to access amenities, relationships and opportunities for employment in a much wider area. Inevitably this both undermines local amenities and favours those who can afford to have access to a vehicle. The sometimes overlooked corollary of 'motoring out' is that it is possible for people to 'motor in' either for some special event, or to patronize a unique amenity or to move in while maintaining employment in an urban context.

The dual reality of the physical mobility enabled by the car, and the virtual mobility made possible by the internet, subtly changes the distinctive culture of rural life, pushing the whole culture, whether urban or rural, towards a similar postmodern and highly individualistic culture. The erosion of close family and community bonds that have existed in rural life for centuries might not be as acute as in some urban areas but arguably it is a growing theme.

Writing in the *Independent*, Richard Askwith reflects on this theme:

> In Wootton, Joan Thomas remembers a village that had a baker, a butcher, a shoe-mender, two shops, a farm, a nursery, a mill, a wheelwright, a glover, a carpenter, a policeman with his own police house, and four pubs. Today, it has one pub, one shop and no active farms. Only a few representatives remain of the old, intermarried families – Bugginses, Gubbinses, Caseys, Davises – who once were the village. Joan is realistic. 'You can never go back to the village you knew as a girl. You have to adapt.' Yet there is something disturbing about the thought that so much has passed away so quickly.
>
> Ronald Blythe, the great chronicler of East Anglian rural life, put it like this when I spoke to him: 'The old traditional village life has almost gone, and so swiftly, and has been replaced by 21st-century technology and comforts that are much the same nationwide, whether one lives in the town or the country. Everybody now has television, everybody has fitted carpets, everybody more or less has a computer, everybody has foreign holidays. It is quite amazing to someone like myself who, as a boy, saw the old harvests, and the old poverty – the good and the bad, all more or less vanished.' [1]

Alan Smith, when he was Bishop of Shrewsbury, commented on this idealized notion of the village. He ends his description with these words:

> Virtually everyone works on the land or in associated roles, such as the blacksmith or the miller. It is a community where everyone knows and supports one another. We know this exists because we have seen pictures of it on the front

of biscuit tins and have watched it on the television as Miss Marple solved murder mysteries.

But, of course, most of this is fantasy, far removed from the complex reality of contemporary rural life. Such idealized villages hardly ever existed. Indeed, many rural communities were not villages at all but scattered farms and cottages, where people lived miles from their nearest neighbour; others dwelt in hamlets that were nothing more than a group of houses or smallholdings with no public buildings or services. In the larger communities, people may have known everyone but they still belonged to networks within their community. Some people, for example, were 'church', while others were 'chapel'; some belonged to the Mothers' Union, others were pillars of the Women's Institute, busily making jam and singing 'Jerusalem'; and the regulars at the pub were hardly ever regulars at the chapel.[2]

Alan Smith goes on to suggest that the rural scene consists of a mix of three groups of people: the first being those who earn their living from farming; the second, those he calls 'the villagers', who have long-standing connections with village life but who do not earn their living from farming; and, finally, those he describes as 'incomers' – and that is not just to do with the time of their arrival but their reasons for coming to the countryside and their ongoing relationships, either economic or social, with those outside of village life. Even within these categories there can be widespread differences in different parts of the nation. For example, in some parts of England, farming is primarily mixed and dominated by family farms, whereas in other parts the farms might be arable, bigger and owned by large conglomerates. The extent to which these three groups either predominate or connect with one another has a significant impact on the character and culture of the countryside.

In some ways, the life of the rural church has similarities to that of the urban in that congregations are small, and that has an impact on resources of finance and leadership. The greatest difference, however, is that of population density and therefore potentially of remoteness and isolation.

Sally Gaze, in noting the recent government categories of settlement form, sparsity or remoteness and function (primarily economic), comments that the combination of these factors can be so vastly varied that it is difficult to characterize rural life in neat descriptors.[3] Nevertheless, she also goes on to comment that there are certain unique elements, and one of those that she chooses to describe relates to the embodiment of a value set that has been more widely lost in our society. Those values relate to a wonder at creation and a commitment to the stewardship of the land. She notes that these are often the people 'who have cared for the same land for generations.'[4] That connectedness with a community gives this sector an influence and importance that may be out of proportion to the number of people in it.

Gaze adds tourism to Alan Smith's categories of rural life. Arguably, those who cater for tourists (and the tourists themselves) could be contained in the category of 'incomer', but actually the transient nature of this numerically and economically significant group of people also impacts the nature of some rural communities.

While it is true that we often describe rural life in terms of its unique characteristics and differences from urban and suburban life, Gaze points out that there are certain national trends that have impacted life in the rural scene just as much as other parts of national life and culture. She outlines seven of these trends, which are listed below, while at the same time noting that these trends sometimes have a slightly different feel in a rural setting. Gaze's trends are as follows:

- Greater mobility.

- Employment changes (primarily more women in the workforce and working away from the home – in farming communities, women were always part of the workforce but were still closely connected to home, as indeed were men).

- Divorce and changes in family life.

- Weakening neighbourhoods.

- The power of networks.

- A consumer culture.

- The death of Christendom (in the countryside the sense that the church belonged to the people has largely been lost.)[5]

Another publication adds one more category to those that Sally Gaze and Alan Smith utilize, and that is migration from overseas. In some rural areas, temporary migrant workers have become permanent residents working both on farms and in related processing industries. Their presence adds a further set of complications because their connections are very distinct within their immediate context of work and accommodation and remain very strong with their home countries. It is too soon to know whether a significant percentage of those who are providing their much-needed labour to the rural workforce will remain in the long term. There are those who suggest that the children of these migrants are becoming well integrated into the broader community in which their families now live, and that indeed the future of these migrant communities may well depend on the effectiveness or otherwise of the Church's mission among them.

New forms of ministry

So how does the Church exercise ministry in a rural setting? One of the rural myths addressed by Alan Smith was the idea that at one time every village had its own resident parson. The reality is 'the creation of hundreds of multi-parish benefices and rural team and group ministries'.[6] Closely connected to the myth of a vicar in every village was that of a time when rural churches were all full. Smith comments:

> Despite the folk memory of many older people who claim to remember a time when their church was full twice every Sunday, an examination of the church registers shows that this was not so in the vast majority of cases ... Churches, of course, may have been full for special occasions, such as village funerals, harvest or Christmas, but research is unanimous in showing that few churches were packed every Sunday. The majority were only partly full – and there were times when some were almost empty.[7]

But even if the idea of a past era when churches were full is indeed a myth, it is certainly true that attendance in the churches in rural areas has declined in recent decades. Moreover, the average age of churchgoers in rural areas is much older than the population at large, and some of their expectations can lead to immense pressure on the existing clergy. Although there are some indications that the decline of previous ages has 'bottomed out',[8] still the pressures on clergy are considerable. Christopher Rutledge writes:

> The present study indicates that there are a significant number of clergy working in rural ministry, who are suffering symptoms associated with emotional exhaustion and feelings of lack of personal accomplishment. In practical terms those clergy experiencing symptoms of burnout are more likely to show a subtle disengagement with those traditional roles associated with rural parochial clergy. In a situation where the majority of rural clergy are responsible for three or more parishes in their benefices it can come as no surprise that many of the clergy feel over-worked, frustrated in their ministry and 'used up' at the end of the day.[9]

The same article includes the result of an in-depth series of interviews with 11 church leaders, and Rutledge comments:

The eleven church leaders spoke of those in rural ministry feeling marginalized by the communities that they serve and feeling pressurized by the unrelentingly high expectations of those who attended their churches. Even people who rarely attended church saw their 'vicar' as a significant person in their village and expected him/her to be constantly available for village events. There was also a constant demand for clergy to operate in liminal areas, where issues of life and death were being faced ...

All eleven church leaders stated that clustering churches and/or parishes in rural areas and bringing them under the responsibility of fewer clergy made the burden of higher expectations even worse. One church leader highlighted the link between the reduction in the number of rural clergy and the weakening of particular village communities where there is now no resident member of the clergy.[10]

Not that there was once a golden age for clergy either. In describing the past, Alan Smith points to a degree of anti-clericalism in rural life:

There have been periods when the Church was not merely un-popular, but experienced considerable grassroots opposition. Historically, it is clear that anti-clericalism was a strong contributory factor fuelling the Reformation. The enforced payment of tithes was a frequent cause of resentment in rural areas, especially when there were poor harvests. This was a significant factor in the growth of the Quakers in England in the mid-seventeenth century. Conflicts were also common when, to give a third example, Methodist preachers were setting up new congregations in villages in opposition to the established Church.[11]

The class divide between the landed gentry and those who worked on the estates was also a factor in fuelling the church and chapel divide. Today, for many reasons, the sharp division between non-conformist chapel life and that of the established Church is nothing like as sharp as it once was. The ease with which Christians feel able to cross the denominational divide has helped enormously in providing gifted and able lay leadership to many village churches.

That crossing of the divide has not been one-way traffic in favour of the Church of England, though in reality the relative determination of the established Church to maintain a presence in every village has meant a stronger 'on the ground' witness for the Anglican Church. Yet even so, there are some significant local situations where the non-conformist presence remains significant. Moreover, there is some evidence that denominations and networks of new churches that have not previously had a rural presence of any significance are beginning to imagine what that could look like. In other words, there is a recognition that it is not sufficient to encourage those in rural areas to commute to nearby towns for worship. The local context really matters.

Caroline Hewlett comments:

> Rural worship is, for the most part, ordinary, yet particular because it is connected to its local community, whose members recognise its value and its part in the identity of that place. The knowledge that worship continues regularly on their behalf and in their community is usually enough for most people, although they may take a more active part when worship connects directly with their lives, through baptisms, weddings, funerals and festivals ...
>
> Worship in rural churches is rooted in the ordinary – and the ordinary, when rooted in the place of worship that belongs to generations of a community, becomes important and holy.[12]

The availability of gifted lay people has been given momentum in most denominations, who have realized that they have to find ways of recognizing ministry beyond that of the full-time stipendiary ministry. Alan Smith describes the response of the Church of England to this need:

> One of the significant developments in ministry over recent decades has been the rapid growth in non-stipendiary ministers, of which there are about 3,000 in the Church of England. In addition, the ranks of readers (formerly known as lay readers) have grown to about 10,000, and in the past 15 years there has been a mushrooming of diocesan schemes to select and train people in other ministries. For example, in the Diocese of Lichfield lay people can now undertake a period of training, equivalent to that of a reader, in the areas of Preaching and Leading Worship, Outreach, Pastoral Care, Prayer Guidance, Youth and Children's Ministry, and Pioneer and Fresh Expressions Ministry. They are commissioned in the cathedral each year at the same time as the readers. Indeed, such is the growth of lay ministries that John Saxbee, the Bishop of Lincoln, believes that there is more ministry going on today in the Church of England than there has been for many decades. However, in terms of stipendiary clergy, virtually all rural churches have to share their priest. In the more remote areas, he or she may have responsibility for up to 14 churches.[13]

The combination of increased stress on clergy and the availability of other kinds of ministry has enabled churches of all denominations to become very innovative in terms of what church actually looks like on the ground. Sally Gaze, in *Mission-Shaped and Rural: Growing Churches in the Countryside*, gives many accounts of innovation on the ground, which really amounts to forms of church planting or Fresh Expressions of church. In describing some of these new worshipping communities, she also explains why they are necessary. In essence, the issue is one of accessibility. It is not the case that people in rural areas (or anywhere else for that matter) have rejected faith in God or belief in the Christian message, but there are a host of barriers that prevent them from becoming part of existing communities, especially in rural areas where traditional worship is the preferred expression of the small number of people who do attend, who are committed and without whom the existing church would almost certainly close.

Sally explains that the barriers can be as varied as difficulty in understanding what is actually taking place in the service, the lack of facilities for children (and the lack of other children for that matter), the fact that most of the congregation are elderly, the lack of heating, toilets, kitchen and other facilities that most community centres would regard as basic needs, the timing of the services and generally worship as an event that reflects a culture that has passed or is passing.

One particular situation featured a successful Alpha course run by the parish church, which saw a number of people come to an expression of faith who then found it difficult to equate what happened in the local parish Sunday worship with the structure and ethos of the group in which they had come to faith. It was necessary in that case to develop a parallel structure, not in opposition to the parish church but as part of their life and witness. One of the powerful reasons for this step was that many in the group expressed that, even though they might persevere with the regular Sunday worship and eventually be able to understand it, they did not feel that they could invite anyone else to attend, whereas they could invite friends to the more informal context that they were beginning to create.

New ways of connecting

Regardless of denomination, the changing structures of ministry are tending to produce different ways of connecting within given denominations. Effectively, the deanery structure in the Anglican Church, the Circuit in the Methodist Church, and newer structures such as multi-site congregations in some more recent expressions of church, all offer an ability to offer resources while at the same time taking account of the unique contours of the local context.

Sally Gaze talks about the multi-parish benefice, which although not necessarily as large as some deaneries, could be close to such a model. She writes:

> In my own benefice, each of the six villages had a rector of their own within living memory. There is now one full time and one half time priest – a quarter of the number of clergy while the population has grown. Because rural parishes have relatively small populations they have been joined together to share an incumbent, but the various parish churches retain separate parochial church councils and electoral rolls. Nobody would claim that multi-parish benefices were designed with mission in mind, but they have their advantages: there is a fond remembrance of what the vicar used to do, together with an awareness that clergy today are more thinly spread and cannot do it all. At best, this results in each church community feeling a strong responsibility for mission and pastoral care within their own parish. Secondly, in a happy multi-parish benefice, there will be a valuing of each other's different styles and an appreciation that while each small church has not got the resources to touch all the different cultures, needs and preferences in their own parish, across the benefice it is possible to develop a variety of mission initiatives and styles of worship. If local church members have already experienced that their church is in creative partnership with other churches in the benefice, starting a fresh expression of church with new Christians who do not find it easy to relate to the existing congregations can seem like the most natural thing in the world.[14]

New forms of partnership (ecumenical co-operation)

The rethinking of structures within denominations is increasingly being mirrored by partnerships across denominations. It is important to note that this is not the same thing as endeavouring to create structures that have the end goal of a single united church. There is a good deal of evidence that the closure of churches to facilitate a single united church, while having some advantages in terms of physical, financial and personnel resources, usually results in a small overall number of worshippers, with many choosing not to join the new united congregation. Long term, the decline continues, and so, while the problem of creating new life, growth and mission is deferred, it is not solved by simply creating a single congregation. Worse still, while the lesson is being learnt the existing congregation is growing older.

The ecumenical co-operation that is emerging is mission-based not structure-based, though obviously structures are involved. One example is the initiative that is sometimes referred to as 'Humber to the Wash'. It currently uses the working title of Lincolnshire FEAST. The website gives the following descriptor:

About the FEAST
The overall vision is to see the further establishment of the kingdom of God in the Humber to the Wash region such that the region is transformed by the love and power of God. To see the kingdom further established could be expressed as:

- people entering the kingdom and joining the kingdom community;
- communities of the kingdom set within the communities of our area, living out kingdom values and demonstrating the life of the kingdom;
- the values of the kingdom becoming the foundations of society and so changing culture.[15]

This vision is subscribed to by a wide range of denominations and networks that range from the Roman Catholic Church to Pentecostal denominations, the Church of England and the Salvation Army. It was pioneered initially by a New Church network called Ground Level and relates strongly to Fresh Expressions.

It takes seriously the rural nature of this region and instead of attempting traditional church plants in every community, looks instead for the founding of an appropriate Christian community in every village or hamlet without prescribing what that might look like. In other words, it uses an incarnational approach to the life of local groups of Christians that takes 'place' seriously while at the same time recognizing that mobility and proximity mean that the notion of 'place' needs to be widened in a rural setting. This perspective is helpfully expressed in *Reshaping Rural Ministry* by James Bell, Jill Hopkinson and Trevor Willmott as 'belonging', which is more than just a settlement:

> Belonging has traditionally been thought of largely in terms of rural settlement or place, but clearly now needs to be expressed in terms of different groups, organizations or networks.[16]

A particular kind of listening is required to take seriously both 'place' and 'belonging' in the context of a given situation. Sally Gaze expresses part of that listening process as follows:

> It is important consciously to take a step back from the things we take for granted to do a third form of listening – listening to God to discern how mission and church should develop in response to the particular cultural context. Many of the 'normal' ways of being church may be part of the answer and may embody essential gospel values – others will look a bit strange and unnecessary when we start to look from the point of view of the people to whom we feel God is sending us.[17]

New forms of mission

Changed forms of leadership, different structures within denominations and across the denominations, suggest that our understanding of mission in rural areas no longer focuses on the maintenance of buildings, still less that of opening many more buildings. But what might mission look like, especially mission that spends time listening to God, taking context and local culture seriously?

As we have already seen, those with a passion for mission, whether in the form of evangelism, church revitalization, church renewal or church planting, often realize that the rural scene is different from urban and suburban settings and that less attention is sometimes paid to it. The failure to take the needs of the rural situation seriously is mirrored in secular as well as ecclesiastical life. From broadband to banks and housing to health, the needs of the rural scene are distinct and often unaddressed.

Again, as we have noticed, as in the inner city, the Church in the rural situation is in difficulty, though for very different reasons. How does one engage in mission in a situation where people are asking spiritual questions, are often deeply conservative in their social attitudes and yet are disconnected from the historic or inherited modes of church? Let's look at an account of one mission initiative, this time undertaken within the Church of Scotland.

For family reasons, Alistair and Ruth Birkett arrived in the border region of Scotland, where the connections with England are both fluid and strong. This is where Ruth's family maintained a family home and for a period at least the family needed Ruth and Alistair's help. Alistair and Ruth had been involved in ministry for some years, but now that kind of leadership was placed on the back burner for a time. They attended the local Church of Scotland but they did not seek to engage in a leadership role.

After a time, the perceptive minister of one of the local parish churches suggested that they might consider becoming

THE PLACE OF THE PARISH

involved in a new programme that the Church of Scotland was pioneering through their 'Emerging Ministries' fund. The fund financed Alistair and Ruth for a five-year period to engage in mission of an experimental kind.

The first year was to be a year of listening to the community. What was God up to in this neighbourhood? That was not an easy discipline for Alistair who was something of an activist and could easily frame what he might do in this situation. The point of the year of listening was to ask questions and particularly to gain a sense of the spiritual journeys that people were engaged in. As they built relationships with people they were able to ask the question, 'What would a spiritual journey look like for you?'

Year two saw Alistair and Ruth initiating a gathering – the Gateways Gathering. This responded to the descriptors of spiritual journeys that people had shared with them. The time, the place, the frequency and the content of the gathering reflected what they had learnt in the listening process.

The experiment is now almost seven years old and a Gateways Fellowship has developed alongside the gathering. The purpose of the Fellowship meetings is to address the spiritual questions that adults in the Gateways gathering are asking. In practice it acts as a discipleship process.

At this stage there is an expectation and the beginnings of a plan to replicate the Gateways expression of church beyond the initial neighbourhood to other parts of the border region. It is not particularly important to talk about numbers at this stage, but two points are worth noting. First, there are more people involved in the Gateways structure than are involved in the two local parish churches nearby. Second, these are mostly younger families who have not been connected with the existing churches. In other words, new ground is being broken, and new people contacted, and notably people from a generation not connected to the existing church structures.

As you might imagine, some of those in the existing churches want to know when those who attend the Gateways gatherings are going to come to the parish church, or 'proper church' as they see it. In reality that will probably not happen, but still this new generation of growing believers might yet turn out to be the new church as the existing church continues to fade away. What that might look like in detail has yet to be addressed.

Curiously, despite the reluctance of many outside the church to attend the existing structures, the connection with the Church of Scotland was vital for Alistair in terms of gaining acceptance from those he was speaking to. The historic Church may not be attractive to the many who do not attend, but it still has social credibility.

The aspect of listening to what God might be up to is always crucial. In talking specifically about rural ministry and the new shape it needs to take, Bell, Hopkinson and Willmott quote Alan Roxburgh and Fred Romanuk's emphasis on listening.[18] They note their encouragement to listen in such a way that we begin to cultivate a new culture and imagination within the church. The Luke 10 passage that describes the sending out of the 70 is key in helping to describe this process. This is a practice more than a principle, yet it highlights the spiritual gift of remaining. For some of us that is sometimes about returning or re-entering the neighbourhood, and it is to this theme that we now turn.

Notes

1 Richard Askwith, 'Another Country: Whatever Happened to Rural England?', the *Independent*, 31 March 2008, www.independent.co.uk/news/uk/this-britain/another-country-whatever-happened-to-rural-england-802653.html.

2 Alan Smith, *God-shaped Mission: Theological and Practical Perspectives from the Rural Church* (Norwich: Canterbury Press, 2008), p. 3.

3 Sally Gaze, *Mission-shaped and Rural: Growing Churches in the Countryside* (London: Church House Publishing, 2006), p. 17.

4 Gaze, *Mission-shaped*, p. 18.

5 Gaze, *Mission-shaped*, pp. 23f.

6 Smith, *God-shaped*, p. 17.

7 Smith, *God-shaped*, p. 15.

8 Smith, *God-shaped*, p. 29.

9 Christopher J. F. Rutledge, 'Burnout and the Practice of Ministry Among Rural

Clergy: Looking for the Hidden Signs', in Leslie J. Francis and Mandy Robbins (eds), *Rural Life and Rural Church: Theological and Empirical Perspectives* (Sheffield: Equinox, 2012), p. 323.

10 Rutledge, 'Burnout', pp. 342f.

11 Smith, *God-Shaped*, p. 15.

12 Caroline Hewlett (ed.), 'Worship', in *Resourcing Rural Ministry: Practical Insights for Mission* (Abingdon, Bible Reading Fellowship, 2015), pp. 85f.

13 Smith, *God-shaped*, p. 18.

14 Gaze, *Mission-shaped*, pp. 97f.

15 FEAST: http://109.104.89.222/feasts/lincolnshire or https://sites.google.com/site/lincsfeast.

16 James Bell, Jill Hopkinson and Trevor Willmott, *Re-shaping Rural Ministry: A Theological and Practical Handbook* (Norwich: Canterbury Press, 2009), p. 10.

17 Gaze, *Mission-shaped*, p. 25.

18 Alan J. Roxburgh and Fred Romanuk, *The Missional Leader: Equipping Your Church to Reach a Changing World* (San Francisco, CA: Jossey-Bass, 2006),pp.2–3.

7

Rediscovering the Local

Lesslie Newbigin began his seminal work *The Other Side of 1984* with the immensely creative question, 'Can the West be converted?' It was a question that had been posed to him by an Indonesian Christian who knew the West very well. He had been able to see something about Western culture that few who were living in the West could see. The question was not 'How can the West be converted?', which is often the way that those who live within that culture read the situation. It was a much more fundamental concern about the unconscious ways in which Christians have been deeply influenced by an Enlightenment culture that assumes that man is the primary agent and God is somehow in the background. Newbigin's Indonesian interlocuter had spotted that the Western world, including the Christian world, had lost sight of the idea that God, not man, might be the primary agent.

That single reality has shaped the way in which Western Christians approach every problem. The question is how to shift the imagination. Alan J. Roxburgh, in his book *Missional: Joining God in the Neighborhood*, describes a conversation that a colleague of his – Mark Lau Branson – had been conducting with a local group of Christians on the west coast of America. Roxburgh says this:

> Mark's comments illustrate how we all live inside a particular story that tells how the world works and how we ought to live in it. In this case a group of Christians that began with

the idea of shaping their church around their neighborhood quickly discovered that they were actually shaped by another story that cut through this ideal. This other story had to do with being individuals who, first, make their own personal, private choices and, second, determine how church might or might not impact these primary choices.

None of us decided at some point in our childhood or young adulthood that we would live inside a certain story of individualism or consumerism or careerism. We were born into a culture that was already shaped by these story elements and we simply assumed them as the normative way of being human and living with one another. In other words, we are all born into some kind of story that already exists, one that shaped us from the moment of our birth. Some describe this as a cultural story.[1]

In describing the problem in this way, Roxburgh explains that he is drawing on the work of the philosopher Charles Taylor, who speaks about the way in which 'social imaginaries' shape our thinking without us necessarily being aware of what is taking place. The example that Roxburgh uses is that of the word 'community'. It's a great Christian word and we often use it to talk about the life of the church, the local neighbourhood, the way in which community has been lost and how we would like to restore a degree of community as we work with the wider neighbourhood.

However, what we cannot necessarily see is that even the way in which we speak about community might be very different from the image held by others about the nature of community. We are often unable to see the extent to which the radical individualism that pervades our culture has in fact evangelized us and limits how we imagine community, still less live it. To quote Roxburgh again:

Mark Lau Branson and his friends in Oakland, while

motivated by communitarian ideals of the New Testament, discovered that a whole other imagination was also at work. Mark described this other imagination as 'consumerism ... shaped by such priorities as individual choice, personal affectivity, and expectations (imaginations) that emphasized the pursuit of careers that should supply meaning and resources for our lives'.[2]

Taylor describes a social imaginary in terms of what seems to be just self-evident ways of living:

> This assumption of individualism is an example of a social imaginary. We don't go around claiming we are self-actualizing individuals. In fact we use the language of community with one another as Christians. We use this public discourse as if it actually shaped our lives when, in reality, a whole other 'operating' system of individualism is at work determining our choices and actions.
>
> In the parable of the three friends, in the way the missional conversation has been shaped in North America, we remain captive to a social imaginary that puts the church at the center of our focus and actions...All the talk about becoming externally driven or missional *churches* only intensifies a captivity to a social imaginary contrary to the movement of God.[3]

Alan Roxburgh and I have written more extensively about this set of issues in *Practices for the Refounding of God's People: The Missional Challenge of the West*. At a recent conference, I was invited to give a synopsis of the main ideas in the book. That was a fascinating experience. I attempted to explain the whole notion of our Enlightenment approach to life – namely, analyse the problem, understand it, come up with a solution and apply that solution. I suggested that this approach places man at the centre, with God at the periphery. Even though Christians might invoke the help of

God, to some extent through our prayers, we have a deep sense that somehow this is all up to us, and God is very substantially absent.

I went to on to explain an alternative approach but, even as I was explaining that alternative, I could see that those who were listening were in fact reworking my explanation in precisely those same Enlightenment categories. In other words, here was someone's attempt (mine in this case) to analyse a problem, to understand it, and to find solutions that needed to be applied. The fundamental question that Lesslie Newbigin had raised, 'Can the West be converted?', had once again been reduced to 'How can the West be converted?'

There remains a tendency to hear the concerns about mission in the West and then to seek to reduce these complex issues to a search for a technique. Almost a case of 'Never mind the problem, what's the answer?' Of course, there is a place for techniques, for action and for insight into the nature of a problem but the missiological challenge that we face cannot be responded to simply by the application of techniques, strategies and plans. Something deeper needs to take place and that something needs to connect with the neighbourhoods in which we are located.

The intention of Mark Lau Branson and his group of committed friends in Oakland was the right instinctive move, but – as many thousands have discovered – this is not an easy thing to do. On the other side of the hyper-individualism of Western culture, there is much to learn and much to unlearn. As we noted in the earlier chapter on the urban scene, there was a time when the level of trust between local communities and the church was deep and lasting. It was almost as if a community could not function well without a number of churches to give hope, opportunity and dignity to those who lived in the neighbourhood.

So when did this mutual affinity break down? For some working-class neighbourhoods, the fracturing of the relationship was evident in the late nineteenth century, but for most towns and cities, and indeed rural settings, we can say that the relationship was intact – if a little strained – at least until the end of the 1950s. In some parts of the West we can say that it lasted longer than that. Certainly in the Celtic nations of the UK, the bond was still unbroken well into the 1960s.

I happened to live in Scotland from the early 1950s until the mid-1960s. The town in which my family lived was one of Scotland's new towns, which had seen a mass transplantation of people from the slums of Glasgow to the new housing and other new amenities of a planned town. The expectation of the development authorities was that the provision of schools, shops, play areas and good-quality housing would by itself develop community even though people had been displaced and disoriented by the move away from extended family networks and friends elsewhere.

The reality was somewhat different. It was a time of anguish for many, and the churches provided the social structures to help rebuild community in a very impressive way. It was evident that there were high levels of trust between church and people. At that time, it was possible to observe that almost everyone identified with a Christian community of one kind or another. The divide between Protestants and Catholics was sharp and meaningful, exacerbated by segregated schools, social clubs and football teams. But none the less, most people could tell you what church they belonged to even if they did not attend – and they knew which church they were *not* going to!

In such a context, the level of trust between church and community was high, and Christian values of kindness, goodness and compassion could be seen to operate. This was not a highly individualistic neighbourhood. People looked out for one another and for each others' children in a way that, if repeated today, might end in court proceedings. Those who were clergy had high social status and the churches were well represented and consulted in civic life. This, we can say, is what Christendom looked like and felt like.

By the time our family moved to England in the mid-1960s, Christendom - at least in England - had all but vanished. It was a shock. We had moved 300 miles in terms of geography but from one age to another in the space of a few hours. Whereas all my school friends in Scotland had been at least nominally connected to a local church, almost none of my new school friends in England were. Neither they nor their parents went to church, nor could they really imagine any reason why they would want to.

That lack of interest was expressed in terms of the Church being irrelevant to everyday life, but in reality something deeper was going on. Church, Christianity, the Bible, the belief system that had created Christendom was no longer seen as credible. The Christendom sense of accepted values no longer served to meet the highly individualistic, consumerist and careerist aspirations of those with whom the churches used to connect. A sudden, dramatic and almost fatal rupture in the relationship between church and people, between congregations and neighbourhoods, had occurred.

To make matters worse, church congregations had little conception of what had happened. It was a dramatic shift in culture that had been growing slowly under the surface and then had suddenly erupted, leaving churches feeling isolated from the neighbourhoods they used to serve. All too often the only conversation that churches had with their immediate neighbourhood was the puzzled question, whether articulated or merely felt, 'Why don't you come to our church any more?' That was not a very creative question, but it demonstrated the feelings of helplessness that many church leaders and ordinary members felt.

In the last two decades of the twentieth century, amid the soul-searching that was taking place among church leaders, there came a quest for solutions. How could the congregations become more effective? There were many attempts to answer that question, ranging from the Church Growth Movement,

Cell Church, Seeker Sensitive Churches, the Purpose Driven Church, the Toronto Movement and many more. Many of these initiatives came from the United States. Most centred on programmes, and how to grow the Church. The shorthand descriptor for these programmes was that of 'attractional church'. In other words, how does one attract people to come to churches, often large churches, essentially with little regard for the context from which people might be coming? This was an extension of evangelism and not an expression of mission.

One of the problems with this approach was that these larger successful churches often depended on a unique set of circumstances for their success – gifted leadership, a significant resource base and, usually, though not always, a suburban or city-centre setting. These factors could not easily be replicated by many other congregations, simply because the unique set of circumstances were precisely that – unique!

Often those who attended such churches travelled from their context to a building that was not primarily concerned with its own local surroundings. This led to the complaint that smaller churches that were attempting to connect with their neighbourhood were losing members to these larger churches and in some cases were closed because of their proximity to them. It caused some to comment that this was not in fact church growth but simply a rearrangement of people who were already Christians. The cynical suggested that existing, committed Christians were moving to situations where they could be better entertained.

That might be a harsh judgement but the issue of incarnational connection to an immediate neighbourhood is an important one that has begun to be addressed by 'attractional' churches in some interesting and creative ways. We will return to that issue in the final chapter of this book.

In the meantime, there were those who had come from some large churches who were beginning to look for more community-based solutions. On both sides of the Atlantic, in North

America and in Europe, churches have been drawn towards creative neighbourhood conversations in a whole variety of ways. A number of people recognize that this is a grass-roots movement, and various attempts have been made to try and identify individuals, locations and stories where neighbourhood and place are being taken seriously in the endeavour to engage in authentic mission. One of those initiatives, operating in the United States, Canada, Australia and the United Kingdom is the New Parish Movement, pioneered by Paul Sparks and Tim Soerens. Paul in particular has been on a journey from a large attractional church to a more neighbourhood-based expression of church. Together with a third colleague, Dwight Friesen, they have captured their story in their book, *The New Parish: How Neighborhood Churches are Transforming Mission, Discipleship and Community*. Paul's story is recorded in this way:

> Paul Sparks had been pastoring a rapidly growing church. It was a GenX church born out of the early nineties Seattle grunge era. Beginning as a college-age ministry, it featured alternative worship bands and more pop culture references than you could shake a stick at. Throughout the years there were truly incredible seasons of awakening and renewal, but Paul was feeling a deep angst. There seemed to be a progressive infatuation with stagecraft and putting on a performance at the gathering. Meanwhile, there was a shrinking connection with what it meant to be the church together in the everyday realities of life.[4]

At the same time that Paul was on his journey, Tim Soerens, who had been experimenting with neighbourhood expressions of church, was discovering that this was not an easy option. *The New Parish* presents Tim's story in this way:

> During this same time, Tim Soerens, who had pioneered a number of missional experiments, was beginning a

neighborhood-based church expression in South Lake Union, in the north part of Seattle. As the months went by, Tim found himself in a bind. On the one hand, he was invigorated by the abundant potential for the church's engagement within the complex dynamics of a rapidly changing urban neighborhood. On the other hand was the massive challenge of helping a church move from coming into the neighborhood with various projects and services, to developing a rich practice of relational life as neighbors living together.

Tim's longing was for relational engagement in the neighborhood and a missional focus organized around holistic neighborhood renewal. Soon he found himself participating in just about every facet of the community's life and growth. He was asked to sit on multiple civic boards stewarding the future of the neighborhood, and helped to build teams for a new farmer's market, advocacy group and community center. Meanwhile, he was inventing experiences that might draw the church into more participatory and engaging ways of living out their faith in the neighborhood together.

But the church was brand new, and very few people began in the neighborhood – and fewer still were able to move in. They hardly had time to get to know each other, let alone the neighborhood at large. Trying to play the role of community developer alone, while pastoring a group of people who hadn't really come to see themselves as part of that neighborhood, was impossible for any one person. Tim was left with a difficult burden – seeing the life and possibility the Spirit had sown all about him and feeling the pain of having very few who were able to be present long enough to see it through.[5]

The very fact that those who have pioneered a network of churches involved in rediscovering parish have found this to be difficult is both realistic and reassuring. 'New Parish' is not another strategy, programme or solution for the difficulties of the Church in the West. It is, however, an important learning place, an orientation in which the Church could learn afresh what it could mean to engage in what we might call 'faithful presence', where the spiritual gift of simply remaining, staying and relating over a period of time might turn out to be a prophetic gift for a society that is fluid, restless and rootless.

Some years ago, I met a brother from the Taizé community, and, during a wonderful conversation over lunch, he shared with me that many young people arrived at Taizé each summer, sometimes for a number of years in succession. He recounted that frequently some of these young people would express wonder and amazement that they met the same monks each year. 'You are still here!' they would exclaim. The reason for that wonder is that often this was the only point of stability in their lives. Their parents had divorced, sometimes more than once. Their friends had let them down, education and employment had failed to meet the emotional needs of their lives and so they had tended to wander and to drift. The spiritual gift of stability, or remaining, of faithful presence, was precious for them. That's not a programme so much as a vocation, a way of life.

One of the key learning points that of all those involved in networks such as New Parish have discovered is that faithful presence begins by listening to the neighbourhood. That is also the way in which a conversation with a neighbourhood begins, one that moves us beyond the despairing cry of 'Why don't you come to our church any more?'

This was a journey that the congregation of which I am a part began some 20 years ago. The journey began with an intention to plant a congregation on the south side of Birmingham. The congregation began with a small group meeting in someone's home and, after finding a number of different meeting places, finally arrived at a rented room in a community centre located in Bournville.

The centre had been built by the Cadbury chocolate factory

as a social amenity for its workers in the 1920s. The Cadbury enterprise had built a large village in a rural area just outside Birmingham in the late nineteenth century. It was one of a number of attempts by employers who wanted to provide their workers with good-quality homes, schools, shops, churches, parks and other leisure facilities, with the conviction that this was a Christian responsibility, a vocation, that was made possible by the success of the commercial enterprise in which they were involved. The community centre was launched with the slogan 'work and play'. The chocolate factory provided the work element for many in the neighbourhood and they were also anxious to provide good-quality 'play' in the form of sports and other recreational amenities. The building was called Rowheath Pavilion, and part of the Pavilion provided changing facilities for teams using the 30 acres of sports grounds. There was also a significant park that included an outdoor lido for swimming in the summer.

In the late 1960s and early 1970s the factory had largely lost its connection with the Cadbury family and a commercial decision was made to cease direct responsibility for the Pavilion and its grounds. An independent charitable trust was established to operate the Pavilion as a sports and community centre.

The Pavilion had rooms for hire and the church plant rented the main hall on a Sunday for worship. After a few years the charitable trust in question ran out of funds and the church plant was invited to take on the lease on a long-term basis. To the partial surprise of the church, taking on the lease did not result in the immediate growth of the church. For one thing, it took a huge amount of effort to operate and maintain the centre and, for another, the community was not much interested in the fact that a church was located in a building that had largely lost its intimate connection with that community. Not only was this not necessarily good news for the community, it was just not news at all.

After much prayer and thought the church decided to begin

a listening exercise, one part of which was to conduct a survey in the neighbourhood, partly to discover what people thought of the church and partly to understand what those living nearby thought were the needs in the area. The findings made for some sobering reflection. First of all, despite the best efforts of the church to date, very few people in the neighbourhood had ever heard of the church, and a surprising number had no idea what happened in the building; a small number were not even aware that the building was functioning, believing it to be either redundant or closed.

The needs expressed by the community were even more surprising, at least in part. The top need was to see a children's playground in operation. No one in the church had ever had that thought. The second was the need for a place to have a coffee with space to talk with their friends, and a third was perhaps more obvious: youth in the neighbourhood needed some resource as there was little for them to do.

After a good deal of soul-searching the church agreed to lead the community in fund raising for a children's play area located next to the building. At the same time they renovated a room that had been largely unused and launched a café, located within a few metres of the playground. This had an immediate impact in the community. A conversation had begun, small at first but growing. Over time, this little-used facility began to attract significant numbers of people to a wide range of activities, some operated directly by the church but many by community groups or commercial enterprises. After a few years the building was opening from 9.00 a.m. to 11.00 p.m., seven days a week. Today, around 15 years after the opening of the children's playground, some 2,500 people use the building each week for activities ranging from sports groups through to dance classes, language classes, children's programmes, spending time in the café and of course church services. The main hall is frequently used as a venue for weddings, parties and other family celebrations. A farmers' market and outdoor festivals take advantage of the grounds, together with a Street Food Friday event that runs through the summer months.

Soundings taken by the church suggest that the centre is now much better known in the neighbourhood. The church is well known and can even echo the words of Acts 2, that they enjoy the favour of the people. A conversation of sorts is in place and within that larger conversation are many individual ones about life, faith and the personal needs of those who visit the various amenities.

The church had undoubtedly grown in numbers through this period but for the most part it has grown because Christians who have moved into the area have chosen to make this their home. Some have come to faith through the various conversations and relationships that have been established through the activities of the centre, but the idea that the 'favour of the people' has translated into huge numbers of people coming to faith is certainly not true.

So what was the church expecting to happen as a result of establishing a conversation with the community? To a certain extent there was a hope that the many relationships formed through that conversation would result in people coming to faith in Christ, simply because the gospel is good news. But it is also true that this was an open journey that sought to discover what God was up to in the community. That journey is based on the conviction that God is the primary agent of mission. If the attempt to have a conversation with the community is merely an evangelistic technique, then we are implicitly claiming that we are the agent of mission, not God.

There is an inevitable tension contained in any attempt to engage in mission. God calls us into partnership with his missionary agenda, but the spirit of our age tends to marginalize the work and presence of God. To a very large extent, Christians in the West have been unconsciously evangelized by the Enlightenment's emphasis on the centrality of humanity and rational activity in the world. Maintaining the sense that God is the agent, and that we cannot know the outcome of a decision to join God in the neighbourhood, is a fragile exercise, a tender shoot.

Even once a church 'enjoys the favour of the people', this is not a recipe for a community-wide orientation towards that church. It simply creates an open space that was not present previously. Potentially and hopefully it is a creative and fertile space, but it is not a programme. Christians are called to live in that space. To use Newbigin's phrase, the congregation is the hermeneutic of the gospel. That means we attempt to live the gospel in such a way that it can be heard, seen and experienced, however imperfectly.

In other words, we are not, in the first place, attempting a Christian version of community development. This is not an endeavour to develop social capital even though that might be a good thing in itself. These things may indeed happen as a by-product of all that is taking place but that is not the core intent.

Living with this strange mission tension between the conviction that it is God who is the agent and yet, on a day-to day-basis, it is us who do things, is achieved by working out a set of core practices that help to develop the congregation as a witnessing gospel hermeneutic. Alan Roxburgh speaks about that activity in this way:

> I am not proposing we should throw away our traditions. Not for a moment! These traditions carry with them a rich heritage; they shape us in the way of the gospel. It is these traditions that give us a language house within which we live, and we can't pretend or deny that this isn't the case. When I am shaped in the language house of the Apostles' Creed; the daily and weekly reading of the Gospel, the Old Testament, and the Psalms; and the regular gift of the Eucharist, I don't enter the neighborhoods and communities where I live as a blank slate. I am who I am because of all these practices of Christian life within a tradition. We shouldn't give these up.[6]

The point about these practices is that they act as a counter-narrative to the prevailing narrative of our time. That secular narrative, described by Alan Roxburgh and myself as a radically individualistic culture that undoes community and social institutions of all kinds, also tends to detach people from the immediate locale, their sense of place, story and solidarity with any social group. It has left Western society, in the words of the previous Pope, 'without roots'. Writing of the period in the mid-twentieth century when this development had become obvious, Roxburgh comments:

> The primacy of the state, the overarching control of consumer capitalism, and the ascent of the Self remained the driving forces. In this sense, the movement of the 1960s was not new. The Euro-tribal churches on both sides of the Atlantic had been displaced as the centers of social, political, economic, and personal meaning, albeit in different ways. Modernity had begun as a grand experiment that, by the midpoint of the twentieth century, seemed to confirm that life could be lived well without God, and that God could, indeed, be made useful to the new, self-actualizing individual.[7]

Life without God, at least in this new hyper-individualistic form, tended to mean life without each other, without community, without place. But what do we expect to happen as a result of living as a Christian community? Clearly, we do want people to become part of that community, but what happens beyond that is more open as an agenda. We could claim it is the values of the kingdom, the idea that we are not primarily autonomous individuals, but social beings who find their meaning in life lived in relationship with God. The values of goodness, compassion and generosity are, we hope, viral in their impact on the places and parishes where we live out our lives as communities of the King and his kingdom. There are no guarantees about what might happen and, more especially, it is clear that this kind of commitment shapes those who engage in this kind of community formation.

It is also clear that this is costly. We may begin with the joy of the incarnation but in doing so, we cannot avoid the pain of the cross. We have indicated that joining God in the neighbourhood is not a quick fix, it's not a methodology that's all about church; instead, it requires a very long-term commitment and it requires those who are willing to walk the way of the cross.

Notes

1 Alan J. Roxburgh, *Missional: Joining God in the Neighborhood* (Grand Rapids, MI: Baker, 2011), p. 58.

2 Roxburgh, *Missional*, p. 60.

3 Roxburgh, *Missional*, p. 60; emphasis in original.

4 Paul Sparks, Tim Soerens and Dwight J. Friesen, *The New Parish: How Neighborhood Churches are Transforming Mission, Discipleship and Community* (Downers Grove, IL: IVP, 2014), p. 8.

5 Sparks, Soerens and Friesen, *Parish*, pp. 10f.

6 Roxburgh, *Missional*, p. 136.

7 Roxburgh, *Missional*, pp. 61f.

8

Place and Parish, Community and the Cross

Even though it was nearly 40 years ago, I still remember vividly my first week in full-time ministry. A number of thoughts were resonating in my imagination. The first was, 'Most of what I have learnt over the last four years is no help to me in this context'. The second was, 'Where can I find some help to equip me for this situation?'

As mentioned earlier, the context was inner-city Birmingham, a location of significant urban deprivation. The time was the early 1970s and the church was in a housing area that had been recently redeveloped as a part of a slum clearance programme that had begun in the 1950s, moving the original population (and genuine community) to myriad other locations in the city, usually involuntarily.

The very patchy redevelopment, conducted over that 20-year period, did not think of community so much as numbers of people that could be accommodated in high-density housing units (mostly, but not exclusively, high rise). The very basic elements of schools and a few local shops were on offer but that, combined with some windswept, empty and rather bleak 'green' areas, was it. The dominant thinking was that if you provide people with good-quality housing they would respond well and naturally build community. There was very little thought given to the nature of community and how it might actually function.

My wife and I moved into the neighbourhood with two small

children in tow. As part of that experience we encountered first-hand the sense of helplessness or powerlessness that pervaded the community. Some of the frustration was visited on us by our neighbours. Our milk (left on the doorstep by our local milkman) was often stolen and you could never be certain that the petrol in your car would still be there when you came to drive off in the morning. We were not being singled out for special treatment. This was a normal part of the locality's terms of trade.

The city authorities who owned all the local housing stock, every social amenity, and even the green open spaces, were not gifted in the creation of social capital. Our family lived in a housing block that comprised four maisonettes (as they were so charmingly called). It had a common entrance way and communal door. On one occasion when local vandals smashed the communal door and left it hanging rather morosely on its hinges, I thought I would demonstrate some responsibility as a local resident and reported the damage to the city housing authority.

Imagine my surprise when I was given a sharp dressing down for having the audacity to interfere with something that was apparently none of my business. The city owned the block, it was their door, and they would find out themselves if it was damaged and repair it in their own good time. They didn't need interfering busybodies like me who had the privilege of living there to waste their time with information like that.

I began to see why the whole neighbourhood was so depressed. The city had taken responsibility for the environment in which people lived – even the grass was owned by the city – but they simply could not deliver on the responsibilities they had assumed. In the process the city authorities had reinforced the sense of powerlessness already experienced by so many of the poor living in their grip.

Community was in short supply and it was not easy to see where it might come from. The mixture of people moving into the area were either working-class English, those of Irish descent, West Indians or the occasional African and Asian from the Indian subcontinent.

The churches were probably the closest thing to community that existed in the area. The Roman Catholic church was reasonably strong because of the Irish connection but the Anglican church was very weak and, despite the local Church of England primary school, had difficulty filling 20 seats out of the 300 on offer. This did not look like community so much as grim survival.

The Salvation Army sought to meet the needs of the very deprived and the handful of non-conformist churches kept their doors open because those who had once lived in the neighbourhood and had attended the church when it was part of a functioning community continued to commute back to those same churches as senior citizens. This loyal band fondly recalled how life had been in the 1930s when the Sunday school was full and social life was lived in the orbit of a full church calendar.

At that time, West Indian residents who had a churchgoing tradition tended to commute out of the community to Pentecostal churches in other areas where Kingston, Jamaica, could be re-created Sunday by Sunday. They often took the same buses out of the community that had brought the commuting non-conformist pensioners into it.

So what could a clergyperson bring to this situation where there was a scarcity of resources – financial and spiritual? There was a woeful absence of human giftedness and energy on offer. At that time there were two kinds of responses to the needs of the community from the non-conformist churches in the neighbourhood, which could be fairly neatly divided into an evangelical and a more liberal approach.

One church in the community, which would have identified with a liberal theological position, had a very entrepreneurial minister who set about identifying social need and locating funding with which to meet that need. The church he produced by this means was a hive of activity all week. The cash generated by the various programmes certainly helped the church to pay its bills. The community was significantly impacted during his time in office, but unfortunately the church did not grow and, when the next couple of ministers were unable to reproduce the same entrepreneurial spirit and skill, the church was eventually forced to close its doors.

The evangelical approach was to see the community as a recruiting ground from which a viable Christian community could be built. This activity was largely unrelated to the broader community, apart from developing friendships and meeting a limited number of local needs so that more people could be welcomed into the life of the church.

That was essentially the approach that the church I served took, and to a certain extent it worked in that the worshipping congregation went up from around 30 people to just over 100. Offerings increased to the point where viability in terms of paying the basic bills was achieved and a certain number of individuals in the community were undoubtedly helped. But the broader community was essentially unchanged. More problematically in terms of building a genuinely local expression of community, power remained with those who commuted, and those who came from the community were essentially made to feel dependent.

Not surprisingly, many who at first felt so warmly welcomed eventually drifted away, some to other churches and some to no church at all. That church still exists but does not have sufficient members to pay a great deal for ministry, though they do meet the other basic needs that enable them to meet Sunday by Sunday.

So why recount a story that, after all, took place some 40 years ago – almost a working life ago? To some extent I include this story because it can encourage us to see what has been learnt since then.

Engaging with the community

There has been much talk and accompanying action about reconnecting with the neighbourhood or community in recent years. That raises a question as to why such talk is necessary in the first place. The language of reconnection suggests that a connection has been lost. The extent of that loss has been surprising. Even as recently as the late 1950s, the beginning of what Hugh McLeod calls the long 1960s,[1] the church was at the centre of most communities and clergy had social standing. The idea that the church would not form a moral and functional centre for public life was almost unimaginable for most people.

Part of the reason for the church seeming to be at the centre of community life is that for the previous 150 years it had been vigorous in its involvement with the day-to-day life of communities of all kinds. In particular, in many parts of Europe, as the population moved from the countryside to the towns and cities, the church was not only present to offer a narrative of hope to the many dislocated migrants, but in many ways helped to shape the very nature of community itself. Some have argued that the very notion of suburbia was an evangelical idea – the creation of a sanitized form of the countryside, close enough to city centres to provide employment, but far enough away to offer a degree of safety for the healthy development of family life.[2]

In the United States, the Second Great Awakening produced a spiritual impetus that moved with the frontier. As Americans moved west there grew a feeling that a new settlement – town, village or hamlet – could not really be a fully formed community without the church. That outcome was not the result of denominational church-planting strategies so much as an outpouring of the spiritual energies and aspirations of millions of lay people. In both Europe and America we are dealing with spiritual movements of a grass-roots nature.[3]

For 150 years, as a modern industrial society emerged in the

West, the church was the place where leadership was formed, gifts were nurtured (in the case of the African American churches, they were considerable musical gifts), the needs of families were met, social welfare organized, basic healthcare encouraged, education offered and children cared for. The church (or chapel) was the natural place that communities used as a focus for social life.

The Sunday school anniversary was often the best organized festival in the village or locality, and the Sunday school outing often the furthest that many ordinary people ventured out of their community. The travel agent Thomas Cook began life organizing Sunday school outings for churches in Leicester. The church was valued, belonged to the people, was a natural expression of the aspirations of many, and in particular was trusted to shape the horizons of the children of every community. In excess of 75 per cent of children in Great Britain were enrolled in a Protestant Sunday school until the outbreak of the First World War in 1914.[4] As Callum Brown suggests, the loss of this position seemed to be sudden and decisive.[5]

This is not the place to debate the reasons for that disconnection in any detail, although it is probably worth noting that the churches with the greatest community connection in the 1950s were the denominations that identified broadly with a liberal theological tradition. They wished to be relevant to the communities they served and, in many ways, that theological tradition seemed to allow the Church an ongoing voice in the affairs of society.

What may have been missed at the time was that this contribution was increasingly a professional involvement on the part of respected and trained clergy as compared with a more popular connection fired by the spiritual commitments of lay people. As with all such sweeping generalizations, there were many exceptions to this description, but in general a shift had occurred.

A more evangelical tradition had not been in the mainstream

of societal life for at least half a century by the late 1950s. As David Runcorn comments so succinctly:

> For the first 60 years of the last century evangelicals were a beleaguered minority. They kept themselves separate, contributed very little to the political, social or theological debates of their day and were experienced by the watching world as defensive and reactionary.[6]

As he also suggests, the evangelical church has experienced an astonishing renewal throughout the very period when church membership and attendance has been in more general decline.[7] That renewal has been across a wide evangelical spectrum – evangelicals standing in a Reformed tradition, classical Pentecostals and a number of waves of charismatics, some of whom have remained in the historic churches and some of whom have formed new denominations and large independent congregations.

In some cases, there have been some interesting combinations of these traditions in the shape of new denominations with a charismatic experience and a Reformed doctrine. Mostly, that renewal has occurred in settings that have been largely disconnected from local communities. With some notable exceptions to which we will return, these have been gathered congregations of the faithful with little success in serving local communities. In some cases, the very choice of location and building design reflects that intent. Large auditoriums have been preferred, located to allow ease of access for commuting congregations. There are no windows in the main centre, no outlook to the neighbouring community. The rationale for such a windowless environment derives from the need to be able to use data projectors and other production features. The worship experience is an event more like a performance from the platform, with little interaction or involvement from the 'audience' as distinct from a 'congregation'.

Throughout this time there have been some pioneering congregations, often located in situations of urban deprivation, that have signalled a different quality of commitment to the surrounding community.[8] Increasingly, other congregations – and sometimes whole networks of churches – have taken note of what has been achieved evangelistically through such engagement.

These vital experiments have been mirrored by an upsurge in evangelical involvement in a wide range of social agencies, from overseas aid through to social justice campaigns.[9] Concern for the future of children, the poor, the marginalized and the deeply damaged has emerged as evangelicals have rediscovered their own history, social conscience, and indeed the call of the gospel message itself.[10]

There is ample evidence from a range of publications, campaigns and even the creation of new organizations[11] to indicate that evangelicals have developed a new seriousness about how they might engage with their community[12] or 're-enter the neighbourhood', to use the language of Alan Roxburgh.[13] On both sides of the Atlantic there has been a rediscovery of evangelical heroes such as the Clapham Sect and, in particular, William Wilberforce. These have often been the motifs that have been used to weave a more 'this worldly' understanding of the kingdom.

More than method

At one level this is all very encouraging. It is profoundly important for evangelicals to regain the passion for campaigning and societal change for which they were well known in the nineteenth century. However, there are also obvious dangers that accompany this new enthusiasm to engage. It is all too easy at a pragmatic level to interpret engagement as just another programme that will prove to be more evangelistically effective than stand-alone evangelistic courses of which Alpha is one example.

There is a long tradition flowing from the Church Growth movement that suggests that evangelicals have long known that to be effective one has to take 'Presence' evangelism seriously, that relationships have to be built before the gospel can be shared, that the meeting of human need helps to earn the right to speak, that acts of kindness lead people to be more receptive to the gospel. All this is true and yet if that is all that social engagement consists of then one is left with a deep sense of unease. This sounds like an attempt to manipulate rather than to wash the feet of the poor. It can easily become just another methodology to get people through our doors rather than an attempt to express a loving presence in the community.

Not only would this descent into cynical methodology be deeply disturbing from the perspective of the heart of the gospel, but there are a number of other aspects that would call such a collapse into technique into question. In two very significant ways such action risks capitulation to the very culture that we are called to convert. First, modernity has a strong culture of 'technique' at its core. The reductionist heart of reason and science suggests that all problems can be studied and that through careful analysis a solution – whether a programme, a product or a method, or a combination thereof – can be found and applied. A particular and known outcome can be predicted.

Second, one of the gospel's inherent objections to modernity has been that this 'cause and effect' approach to reality not only rules God out of the picture, other than as a distant prime mover, but it also leads to a view of people as objects. The tendency of global capitalism to commodify everything and everyone reinforces the kind of depersonalization of those we are called to love and acts to undermine the very gospel we seek to proclaim. For many good reasons we have to be clear that love can never be a technique. What human relationship could survive such a cynical approach?

Christians are wedded to the idea that the 'other' person with whom we seek to communicate has to be treated with the same deep, unfathomable love with which God treats us. To use Martin Buber's language, the other person is never a statistic or a marketing target and must become for us an honoured 'thou'. In addition, this honoured 'other' has potential insights into the gospel that could only be revealed through them. As our gospel has come to us through Scripture and tradition, but understood through our lives and contexts, so another will encounter the gospel uniquely. Through encounter there is the possibility that we and they will experience God at a new depth. We will both be changed.

The cross has always been at the centre of the evangelical approach to the gospel. But David Runcorn comments that theologically the stress on the cross is now expressed alongside the doctrine of the incarnation,[14] and it is a reaffirmation of the essential connection between these two doctrines that so typifies the recent renewal of evangelical thought and action. It is the model of God's incarnation that underlies evangelism, and that reverence for the person in all their particularity of culture, time and place. The powerless cross models a willing vulnerability in all encounters.

There are techniques, insights, orientations and even programmes that can be taught and that can help us to listen to people and communities. But it is this that is part of our difficulty. For example, we do need to learn how to listen anew, we will do well to learn about team, about the handling of conflict, of how the creative arts can help us to communicate in fresh and dynamic ways. In the same way we can learn to attend to God, to notice God's presence afresh in our surroundings. Choosing to engage with spiritual disciplines has always been a hallmark of the mature Christian. But such fresh learning must never corrupt our basic appreciation of the 'thou', the sacred, the divine in others; indeed, it should assist it.

Power and the meeting of need

In the midst of this new learning, which is powerful and

therefore capable of abuse, we also need to grapple again with the issue of power itself. We have not addressed the question in this chapter as to what happened to the evangelical movement in the nineteenth and very early twentieth century. How could a movement that was so profoundly influential in shaping culture more widely, and local communities so creatively, have lost its influence so suddenly?

I want to suggest that all successful movements find it difficult to deal with the problem of their own success, partly because few of us see success as a problem. The history of mission suggests that just as we obtain our dearest desire (seeing our friends and neighbours, indeed those we never thought would even consider the gospel message, entering the church), at a deep, deep level we are undone, hence the exit of the saints from the church to the desert.

The fundamental point here is that when a lot of people join the Church in a short space of time, they bring their cultural values into it in such a way that the core of the Christian message is compromised, or even lost, under the weight of the external culture.

Is this simply an impossible difficulty for which there is no answer, and which condemns us for ever to a cycle of success, denouement, repentance and recovery? In one way we have to be realistic and say that it does, at least in so far as we have to learn afresh to interpret the gospel in every cultural setting – and culture is never static. But in another sense, we might be able to set the stage in such a way that the learning process is ongoing and complacency is resisted.

We have unearthed two related problems that arise from an abuse of power. The first is commodification, treating people as mere evangelistic targets. The second is a complacent response to influence and impact. I want to propose at least three potential resources and priorities that can help us avoid these dual problems. All three of these resources are aids to the creation of a particular kind of community. This is the heart of the point I want to make.

Our approach to the community we seek to serve can only be kept healthy if the community that does the serving is itself healthy and pays attention in an ongoing and appropriate manner to that same issue of health. Service to others must never deteriorate into an abuse of self or a failure to love oneself appropriately. To put it tritely, we can't love others if we don't love ourselves. What are these resources?

First, theological thought itself is a resource to be rediscovered. Ellen T. Charry has written eloquently on the need for the Church to rescue theology from its academic captivity. For Charry, there is a need for a theology of wisdom or sapiential insight that is valued as much as a theology of issues of truth.[15] The surrender of theology to the categories of the Enlightenment concerning epistemology have rendered it unable to speak about God, and that has left theology wounded and unable to serve either the Christian community or indeed the wider world.

Theology today lives on the margins of the secular culture, the margins of the 'academy', and the margins of the Church. It could be that responsibility for this marginalization lies equally with a desacralized culture and with the field of theology itself. Perhaps the renewal of theology is not unlike the renewal of the Christians about whom our theological teachers worried, as a mother cares for a child who has lost her way in a confusing world. She must be healed before she can flourish again.[16]

How might that healing take place? In Ellen Charry's view there is an issue about the modern values of individuality, autonomy and freedom.[17] These values have Christian roots, but have been cut adrift, acquiring new meanings in the process. So, for her, the Trinity is of immense importance as a theological theme and needs to balance the Western emphasis on the doctrine of the cross. It is the Trinity that allows us to come to what she calls the third pivot of the Christian self, which – as we have seen above – must be grounded in God.[18] She writes:

The third of the three distinguishing pivots of the Christian self is its belonging in the body of Christ. Divine guidance takes place in the community of the faithful. While the secular emancipation narrative encourages the self to free itself from formative and socializing influences that might thwart self-expression, the Christian seeks formation in the midst of an ordered community in order to prepare itself for a cross-defined life that may move across the grain of the dominant culture.[19]

The second resource in the armoury is the recovery of the spiritual disciplines. One of the curious realities about spiritual disciplines is that at one level they insist that we face our own, very individual relationship with God. In that sense we are alone with God. Prayer, periods of intentional silence and listening, reflection on Scripture and fasting all have the potential to throw us into a deep isolation with God. Commodification, complacency and indeed all our ego agendas fall away in the hiddenness of this isolation. And the God we meet in such isolation is a God who is, as God, living in community; and this triune God deals with us in our isolation in such a way that we are impelled to consider afresh our relationship with others. This is not an aloneness that leaves us in isolation. Even the hermit is called to be alone to pray for others, not for himself.

Third, life within the Eucharistic community is a resource. What does it mean to live as a Eucharistic community? Clearly, it must mean more than the simple act of a regular celebration of the Eucharist in a strictly liturgical sense, although it is not for nothing that the Catholic tradition emphasizes that wherever the Eucharist is celebrated, the Church is somehow created. It is also not for nothing that much of the Protestant tradition draws the community together in order to celebrate the Eucharist. The Eucharist, either in creating the community or in giving community a focal point, is always wedded to the idea of community itself.

But the point about the Eucharist in such a setting is that it tells a story that helps us to define something of who we are as a community. It is by living in this story – not this story alone, but this story in particular – that we learn something about how to be a community of God's people able to serve in non-coercive, sacrificial ways that challenge the fundamental forces of evil and call a new reality, a heavenly banquet, into being.

As Stanley Hauerwas suggests, the sacraments enact the story of Jesus, and thus form a community in his image.[20] By re-enacting the Last Supper we are drawn inevitably to the meaning that it had originally for the people of Israel, but also to the meaning that Jesus invested in it. His sacrificial death – or, more precisely, the reality that God himself was going to lay down power, all power, as his response to the violence of evil – crashes in on history as something dramatically different, as a disclosure of the nature of God utterly unlike anything that Israel had experienced previously. This story, above all other stories, calls us to redemptive, costly love in our relationship with our community. Frequent participation in this feast helps to create the kind of community that can never be comfortable with attempts to coerce commitment and belief even if such a thing were ever truly viable.

We are called to live in the story – not our story, but The Story – so that in time, our story becomes ever more closely conformed to The Story.

Notes

1 Hugh McLeod, 'Introduction', in *The Decline of Christendom in Western Europe, 1750–2000*, ed. Hugh McLeod and Werner Ustorf (Cambridge: Cambridge University Press, 2003), p. 18.

2 See Schlossberg on the issue of evangelicalism as the founder and shaper of Victorian society. (Herbert Schlossberg, *The Silent Revolution and the Making of Victorian England* (Columbus, OH: Ohio State University Press, 2000).

3 See Roger Finke and Rodney Stark, 'How the Upstart Sects Won America: 1776–1850', *Journal for the Scientific Study of Religion* 28, no. 1 (1989), pp. 27–44.

4 Callum G. Brown, *The Death of Christian Britain* (London: Routledge, 2001), p. 168.

5 Brown, *Death*, p. 1.

6 David Runcorn, *Spirituality Workbook: A Guide for Explorers, Pilgrims and Seekers* (London: SPCK, 2006), p. 43.

7 Runcorn, *Spirituality Workbook*, p. 43.

8 For example, the Eden Network: http://eden-network.org/.

9 Micah Challenge is an example of an international movement for global justice that arose from within the evangelical context.

10 Tom Wright, *Surprised by Hope* (London: SPCK, 2007), p. 224.

11 For example, Serve (www.communitymission.org.uk) is a new initiative in holistic mission instigated by the Evangelical Alliance. Redeeming Our Communities (www.roc.uk.com) enables local partnerships for community cohesion and transformation.

12 Scot McKnight helpfully describes the shift in the Church from a personal salvation-centred gospel towards a kingdom-focus one. See Scot McKnight, 'Atonement and Gospel', in Kevin Corcoran (ed.), *Church in the Present Tense: A Candid Look at What's Emerging* (Grand Rapids, MI: Brazos Press, 2011), pp. 123–39.

13 Alan Roxburgh, *Missional: Joining God in the Neighborhood* (Grand Rapids, MI: Baker, 2011).

14 Runcorn, *Spirituality Workbook*, p. 43.

15 Ellen T. Charry, *By the Renewing of your Minds: The Pastoral Function of Christian Doctrine* (Oxford: Oxford University Press, 1997), p. 238.

16 Charry, *Renewing*, p. 245.

17 Ellen T. Charry, 'The Crisis of Modernity and the Christian Self', in Miroslav Volf (ed.), *A Passion for God's Reign* (Cambridge: Eerdmans, 1998), p. 95.

18 Charry, 'Modernity', pp. 104–108. The first two of Charry's pivots are dwelling in the dignity of God, and heeding the call and cross of Jesus Christ (p. 104).

19 Charry, 'Modernity', p. 108.

20 Stanley Hauerwas, *The Peaceable Kingdom: A Primer in Christian Ethics*, 2nd edn (London: SCM Press, 2003), p. 107

9

Towards a Re-founding of the Parish

The issue of 'place' has strong connections with identity. The place that we are from or where we still live shapes some part of who we think we are, what we believe, what we value and how we see the world in which we live. David Goodhart has written a book in the wake of the Brexit vote, *The Road to Somewhere*,[1] that attempts to understand the way in which people voted in the 2016 referendum in relation to two categories of people. He calls them 'Anywheres and Somewheres'. His basic thesis is that those who feel they are rooted in a particular place voted very differently from those whose life, skills and education enable them to live anywhere. This, more than any other factor, was the most important defining element in their tendency to vote one way rather than another.

Of course, that definition is not unrelated to class, occupation and opportunity, and in a way that is precisely the point he is wanting to make. He says this:

Only a couple of generations ago, a large number of people performed skilled jobs that required little cognitive ability but required a lot of experience to do well and thus protected the status of those doing them. And those middling, often manufacturing, jobs also offered achievable incremental progression. Now the majority of jobs in Britain either require a university degree or virtually no training at all.

And thanks to residential universities and the dominance of London, cognitive ability and social achievement is associated with *leaving*, separating oneself from one's roots and becoming an Anywhere. (Leavers, meaning people who leave their home town and never return to live there, tended to be Remainers in the EU referendum and remainers tended to be Leavers.)

Today, about three in five Britons still live within twenty miles of where they lived when aged 14 – but few of those people are Russell Group university graduates.[2]

Arlie Russell Hochschild, in her book *Strangers in their Own Land: Anger and Mourning on the American Right, A Journey to the Heart of Our Political Divide*,[3] makes a similar point, though in a much more narrative style, about the divide that has grown in the United States between those who voted for Donald Trump and those who voted for Hillary Clinton.

Goodhart, having made a very strong case throughout his book for the divide between Anywheres and Somewheres, offers an intriguing caveat towards the end of the book. He notes that many Anywheres, despite their ability to live in many locations, nevertheless often desire to put down roots at some point in their lives. Equally, Somewheres are not always as deeply invested in their immediate community as they could be. There is, in other words, a potentially creative space where both these groups might develop a sense of identity if there are other factors operating that would encourage the geographic space where they live to become meaningful place.

In the second edition of his book, Goodhart acknowledges that he gives little space to the importance of faith communities. He says:

Friendly critics pointed, rightly, to the absence of religion in the book and its potential importance as a bridge between the localism of particular religious communities and the universal connectedness of many faiths.[4]

The contribution of faith to the growth of social capital in particular places and communities has previously been well documented by Robert Putnam in his book, *Bowling Alone: The Collapse and Revival of American Community.*[5] That book was followed up by another entitled *Better Together: Restoring the American Community,*[6] co-authored by Lewis Feldstein, which tells stories from around North America of groups rebuilding a sense of place and community. These stories and others remind us that there is some counter-balancing of the trend towards globalization with movements that emphasize localism. That does not eradicate the overall mobility of Western societies but it does offer an opportunity to consider how an immediate sense of place or parish can begin to be renewed.

The authors of *The New Parish* offer some thoughts as to what that might look like:

We are contrasting the new parish with lingering conceptions the church has carried since Christendom, when the institutional church more or less dictated the form of the neighborhood. The church that is emerging in the parish today is different in many ways. The first difference is that the neighborhood – in all its diversity – has a voice that contributes to the form of the church. There is a growing sense that the Spirit works through the relationships of the neighborhood to teach us what love and faithfulness look like in that particular context.

The new parish is also different in the way diverse church expressions with different names and practices are learning to live out their faith together as the unified church in and among the neighborhood. Whereas the old parish was often dictated by a single denomination outlook that functioned as law, the new parish can include many expressions of the church living in community together in the neighborhood. Not only do parishioners learn to love and listen to neighbors from other church expressions in the parish, they also seek out partnerships with people from other faith perspectives who have common hopes for the neighborhood.[7]

So what inhibits congregations from developing a move towards a new parish as distinct from the old parish? The Churches of the West, just like society itself, have lived through a period of enormous change. That change has been sufficiently severe that Churches, both as denominational systems and as individual congregations, are sometimes experiencing the paralysing feeling of shock. It is hard to understand what has happened. Decline has been sudden and deep. The familiar has gone and efforts to find short-term solutions have not worked – and nor can they.

Moreover, the societal changes that have impacted church life have also had similar effects on just about every social structure, whether trade unions, political parties, the Scout Association, community associations, marriage and family life. Any social structure that has been based on solidarity, long-term commitment to a group rather than to a short-term cause, is very hard to sustain. This is a new, puzzling landscape that is difficult to negotiate.

Many churches are simply exhausted and the thoughts of those in leadership turn to survival, and often to retirement for leaders who will leave the task to those who will follow. The problem is that those who follow tend to have very similar thoughts and emotions. Engaging in the kind of developments that the creation of 'new parish' demands is very hard work and the energy to invest in that kind of re-imagining is in short supply. In Chapter 7, we quoted Tim Soeren's experience of running this kind of experiment, and how he found it to be personally challenging. But, more especially, it was difficult for church members to keep pace with that level of activity.

Ministry in all its forms

There is therefore an issue of resources, and so the involvement of lay people in ministry becomes a critical element in creating a structure that we might call 'new parish'. What we are looking for is something that moves beyond the old clergy/laity divide.

Where that divide is deep and clear-cut then lay people tend to become 'volunteers' rather than deeply invested team members. The question becomes not so much 'Do our structures allow lay people to participate?' (they have always done that) but rather 'Can our structures allow lay people to lead, to shape, to re-create the culture of the local church through their active engagement with both church and community?'

What we are describing here is not an insular community composed of those regular worshippers who, while they have a sense of ownership and belonging, are nevertheless holding on to tradition at the expense of mission but rather a community seeking to reinterpret the traditions that are held dear in the context of those who are outsiders. Andrew Rumsey, towards the conclusion of his book on parish, speaks of the strange irony of this kind of posture. He talks about the ways in which the parish brings a broken and divided people into one body:

> It does this only by drawing near those who were once far off – and by seeing neighbourhood as something offered especially by and to the outsider. It is not a little ironic that 'parochial' has come to epitomize insularity and self-containment when its original meaning is far closer to our contemporary definitions of interloper or refugee: but this, at least, is an irony we can work with to great benefit.[8]

As he also notes, the task of expanding ministry, mission and the connection with the outsider has been hugely assisted in recent years by the addition of new types of local ministry associated with Fresh Expressions and mission-shaped church, which offer 'a more contemporary response to the missionary challenges faced by the Church of England.'[9] Similar initiatives have been adopted by other mainstream or historic denominations, while the newer churches or networks, who are increasingly becoming the new mainstream, have tended to be influenced either by the idea of the five fold ministries referred to in Ephesians chapter 5, or by the idea of flat structures, or indeed by a combination of both.

Re-inventing the 'attractional' church

The idea of the local is undergoing a significant renaissance both in the life of the Church and the broader culture, as reflected by such movements as environmental concern. At the same time, there is also a shift in the self-understanding of larger 'attractional' churches, which in the past have tended to draw people out of the local and into worship services that are profoundly disconnected from their immediate neighbourhood.

While we can't argue that this is universally the case among such churches, there are some important indications that there is a move in that direction. The key concept is for larger churches to see themselves not so much as a model for that which is to come, but a resource church for surrounding 'parish' or 'local' churches that are deeply invested in their immediate communities. That represents a significant shift in thinking and to a large extent, at least in England, it has been spearheaded by the dialogue that has occurred between Holy Trinity Brompton, the Church Commissioners and the dioceses who have in the past relied on funds from the Commissioners to underpin churches in needy neighbourhoods.

This is not the place to document that particular debate so much as to highlight the general direction of movement. Whereas in the past, larger churches were simply seen as undermining local churches, it is quite another matter for them to see themselves as churches that resource local churches. To some extent, such a development draws on an older tradition of 'minster' or mission churches that certainly assisted the gradual development of a parish system in the early days of Christianity's growth. In more recent times, denominations, and now new church networks, have often based their growth and structures around large central congregations that were able to resource and encourage church planting both in close proximity to the mother church but also as mission initiatives in completely new areas. The Methodist Circuit and the Baptist District, to name two such structures, were often brought into being by this means.

Larger churches that adopt such a posture tend to move from being 'attractional', in the sense of 'entertaining' or 'amusing' their attendees, towards a stance of equipping, with a view to sending out those same members. Not so much to add and to keep, but to convert and to send. As the theme of mission as a concern that is broader than evangelism begins to emerge, the thinking of larger churches tends to change. The local does begin to become more significant, even within the context of their immediate surroundings.

Black-majority churches

Many of the larger churches in Western cities today are black-majority congregations, often formed from a single cultural group. As we have noted earlier, these congregations are not so much concerned with their immediate 'parish', even though, ironically, one of the largest of the black-majority denominations uses the term 'parish' to denote a local congregation.

One leader from within the black-majority churches outlines a typical four-stage journey for these congregations. The first is simply to survive. At this point there is a desire to gather and to help the members of the congregation cope with their new situation. The second is to grow within their new context, primarily if not exclusively by attracting others from their own culture, nationality and language group. This is a period of becoming established. The third is to help the home country, either with practical resources or by conducting missions in those lands. It is only at the fourth stage that there grows a concern to consider the wider society in which they find themselves. That fourth stage is often triggered by an awareness that their single cultural congregation could easily become a one-generation phenomenon unless they take mission in their immediate context more seriously. Many of these newer black-majority churches in the UK are aware of the cultural isolation experienced by the earlier establishment of West Indian congregations and are anxious not to repeat that experience.

The single biggest catalyst for that change becomes an awareness that their children and grandchildren are not adapting well to the kind of church that they have created. So the question arises, 'What kind of church would be appropriate for our children who are living with a dual-culture awareness?' They know the culture of their parents and in some respects they appreciate it but they are living in a Western culture and that is really their milieu. As some of these congregations give their young people an opportunity to experiment, they sometimes find that they can reach out to their British friends. Most of these friendships have been forged either in schools or in other social settings that are fairly local, or neighbourhood based. At this stage, therefore, some – though by no means all – black-majority churches are beginning to take the local, the parish, more seriously. The neighbourhood in all its diversity now begins to matter.

Despite the astonishing decline of Churches in the Western world, and their perceived lack of vigour and importance from the perspective of public life, it is the case that the ubiquitous presence of the Church, on the ground in virtually every community, remains a fundamental strength. The acknowledged activity of the Church in social action, ranging from food banks, to concern for refugees, prisoners, human trafficking and provision for those with disabilities of one kind or another, is an indication of social capital. However, the decline of congregations is undoubtedly a difficulty – one that is being ameliorated to some extent by the planting of new congregations and the re-planting of some existing ones.

The art of gathering

To re-engage neighbourhoods such that the local, the parish, becomes vibrant again is obviously desirable but not altogether straightforward. Creating the kind of worshipping community that makes for a healthy parish requires a certain kind of charism. Gathering as a Christian community is a skill that needs to be carefully nurtured. We outlined some descriptors of a healthy parish community in Chapter 3 and we warned against seeing these elements as a method or a model. What we are talking about here is the common life that is the basis of parish community and much else besides. The common life implies a gathering of God's people in particular places, not as identical manifestations of a single organization, but as local expressions of something much deeper.

Gerhard Lohfink asks the provocative question, 'Does God need the Church?' He uses this question as the title of his book and, of course, in one way God obviously does not need the Church. And yet there is something about the nature of the triune God that seeks to create a people, and to have fellowship with those people. Lohfink makes these claims:

> Christian faith, just like Jewish faith, subjects *all* of life to the promise and claim of God ... it demands that social relationships must change and that the material of the world must be molded. Faith desires to incorporate all things so that a 'new creation' can come to be ...

> At the same time faith tends toward a more and more intensive communion among believers, for only in the community, the place of this communion, only in the place of salvation given by God can the material of the world really be molded and social relationships really transformed. It would therefore be essential to Christian faith that individual believers should not live alongside another in isolation but should be joined into a single body. It would be essential that

TOWARDS A RE-FOUNDING OF THE PARISH

they weave together all their gifts and opportunities, that in their gatherings they judge their entire lives in light of the coming reign of God and allow themselves to be gifted with the unanimity of *agape*. Then the community would become the place where the messianic signs that are promised to the people of God could shine forth and become effective.

All of this is part of the tendency of the faith to embodiment. Christian faith *of itself* produces an impulse to bind believers in communion and by way of that communion to all spheres of life into God's new creation. This integration tendency is a property of faith itself ...

The communion of believers thus is not something that is merely spiritual and intellectual. It must be embodied. It needs a place, a realm in which it can take shape.[10]

That embodiment therefore is not a convenient way of organizing the people of God. Still less is it merely an evangelistic agency or some other mechanism for performing acts of charity. Rather, as Lohfink suggests, it is the place where the 'messianic signs' might 'shine forth and become effective'. That is a rather challenging concept but these lofty thoughts in fact are made possible in the context of the very ordinary things of life, social relationships lived in the context of failure and disappointment as much as in joy and victory.

In writing about Christian community, Dietrich Bonhoeffer says:

In the Christian community thankfulness is just what it is anywhere else in the Christian life. Only he who gives thanks for little things receives the big things. We prevent God from giving us the great spiritual gifts he has in store for us, because we do not give thanks for daily gifts ... We pray for the big things and forget to give thanks for the ordinary, small (and yet really not small) gifts. How can God entrust great things to one who will not thankfully receive from him the little things? If we do not give thanks daily for the Christian fellowship in which we have been placed, even where there is no great experience, no discoverable riches, but much weakness, small faith, and difficulty; if, on the contrary, we only keep complaining to God that everything is so paltry and petty, so far from what we expected, then we hinder God from letting our fellowship grow according to the measure and riches which are there for us all in Jesus Christ.[11]

It is precisely in the local and the particular that we are able to work out these ordinary relationships in the context of the call of God. And as Bonhoeffer also makes clear, it is all too easy for human dreaming to undermine that call from God. In a curious and arresting statement, Bonhoeffer says, 'God hates visionary dreaming; it makes the dreamer proud and pretentious.'[12] It almost seems like an offensive protest in the context of a society where big dreams and visions are commended, where individuals are encouraged to believe that they can achieve whatever they desire – 'just go for it'. And yet it doesn't take much reflection to see that these efforts at individual self-actualization have little to do with community formation.

Bonhoeffer goes on to say of such visionary dreamers:

He enters the community of Christians with his demands, sets up his own law, and judges the brethren and God himself accordingly. He stands adamant, a living reproach to all others in the circle of brethren. He acts as if he is the creator of the Christian community, as if his dream binds men together. When things do not go his way, he calls the effort a failure. When his ideal picture is destroyed, he sees the community going to smash. So he becomes, first an accuser of his brethren, then an accuser of God, and finally the despairing accuser of himself.[13]

The creation of a worshipping Christian community in the context of the local is a difficult undertaking; none the less, how might it be possible to move in such a direction? Two very basic elements of the Christian call are vital. Both are deeply connected to the notion that we are not just a human community, committed to love but not to truth, but we are called to be a sacramental community. These two dimensions are the decision to be a follower of Jesus, a disciple, connected to the sacrament of baptism, and the day-to-day lived experience of community in the context of the Eucharist. It is baptism and Eucharist that shape us as a local sacramental community. That reality of seeking to be such a community connects the horizontal relationship we seek with others in the local fellowship with the vertical reality of a relationship with God.

We can only live out our relationship with God in relationship with others and, equally, we can only live out a healthy relationship with others in community out of our relationship with God. Bonhoeffer points out that we are called to gather, however difficult that may be:

It is by the grace of God that a congregation is permitted to gather visibly in this world to share God's Word and sacrament ...

The physical presence of other Christians is a source of incomparable joy and strength to the believer.[14]

This is the context, then, in which we live as disciples, having been joined to Christ and to each other in the sacrament of baptism. As Lohfink declares:

An individual cannot first begin to believe alone and then, afterward, join the Church. The acceptance of faith is already identical with incorporation into the church. Accepting faith already means desiring the communion of believers.[15]

It is in the context of the body of Christ that one learns to be a disciple. We can say that the normal experience of discipleship should be that it is conducted in the context of community. Indeed, we could go further and say that it is almost impossible to be 'discipled' as an individual. That sets up a tension with our contemporary, highly individualistic culture that attempts to persuade Christians of exactly that – the idea that one becomes an individual disciple.

Arguably, the dignity of the individual person, their rights and privileges, their gifting, their personality, their uniqueness, their ultimate value, their relationship with God, are all ideas that were introduced by the Christian community to a pagan world that had little regard for human life. Yet our secular world, in cutting the connection between the individual and human community with its associated sense of responsibility to and for others, has done an immense disservice to the individual. We are not intended to be autonomous individuals. We are social beings, intended to live in relationship, just as the triune God does. The recovery of community in the context of the local where we do not choose an affinity group but rather mix with our neighbours – people we do not choose but who are given to us – is an important gift in terms of discovering what it means to be human.

It is important to emphasize that we are not talking merely about the formation of local community as a kind of social club or society, even one with very altruistic aims. That is again to reduce the local church to a merely instrumental purpose. John Zizioulas makes a distinction between Christian community and a secular society. He says:

Contemporary humans live every day under the weight of the opposition between the individual and the collective. Their social choice is not *communio* but *soeitas*. And because there is no other choice, their violent reaction against collectivism leads to individualism and *vice versa*: for, paradoxically the one presupposes the other.[16]

Zizioulas describes Christian community as a Eucharistic community. He says of this community:

> the Eucharist does not offer the world a system of moral rules, but a transfigured and *sanctified* society, a leaven that will lead the entire creation by a sanctifying *presence*, and not by the compulsion of moral commandments. This *witnessing* presence does not force intolerable chains, but *invites* them to the freedom of the children of God, to a communion with God that will bring rebirth …
>
> Why the moral decadence in secular society? Why does our Christian voice resound as if in a vacuum? We have turned to moral preaching and to statements of moral principles to convince the world, and we have failed; no one hears us. We offered the *Logos* and the world did not accept it. We forget that the *Logos* is not our words, but a Person, not a voice, but a living Presence and that this personal presence is embodied in the Eucharist, which is above all *communion* and *assembly*.
>
> This society, which was transfigured in order to transfigure, no longer exists. It was dissolved by our pious individualism, which believed that, in order to work in the world, it had no need for the parish, for the eucharistic community, and it replaced them with an instructive 'logocracy', believing that it would be sufficient to *tell* the world to change. The presence of our Church in the world has become a pulpit without a sanctuary and a group of Christians with neither unity nor community. We do not draw our moral attitudes from the new life that we enjoy as the eucharistic assembly, and society thereby has lost the leaven of the divine communion that, alone, can spark an authentic revival.[17]

Zizioulas is perhaps a little hard on the Church as a whole, though in fact his precise target is more the Orthodox community. But we take his point: the creation of a Eucharistic community or assembly at a very local level, wherever Christians are to be found, is of crucial importance for the future of our civilization and not just the Church. In that vital sense the future of the parish is intertwined with the future of our world. Possibly the most prophetic statement that our hyper-individualistic culture needs is the local reality of communities acting out what it means to love one another, to embrace the needs of the world, to enact truth – all in the context of the Eucharist. This simple act of memory connects the salvific act of Christ upon the cross with a redeeming present and the ultimate community of a new heaven and a new earth.

The rhythm of weekly worship in a local context helps to create the kind of communities that have the innate strength and substance to resist the narratives of our secular age, to produce instead a parish life that is creatively connected to those who live nearby. It enables the local to be connected to the wider body. Our liturgies may be locally expressed in the parish, but they are universally significant in the story they tell to cultures and peoples of every kind.

Notes

1 David Goodhart, *The Road to Somewhere: The New Tribes Shaping British Politics*, 2nd edn (London: Penguin, 2017).

2 Goodhart, *Road*, pp. xivf.

3 Arlie Russell Hochschild, *Strangers in their Own Land: Anger and Mourning on the American Right, A Journey to the Heart of Our Political Divide* (New York: New Press, 2018).

4 Goodhart, *Road*, p. xi.

5 Robert Putnam, *Bowling Alone: The Collapse and Revival of American Community* (New York: Simon & Schuster, 2000).

6 Robert Putnam and Lewis Feldstein, *Better Together: Restoring the American Community* (New York: Simon & Schuster, 2003).

7 Paul Sparks, Tim Soerens and Dwight J. Friesen, *The New Parish: How Neighborhood Churches are Transforming Mission, Discipleship and Community* (Downers Grove, IL: IVP, 2014), pp. 31f.

8 Andrew Rumsey, *Parish: An Anglican Theology of Place* (London: SCM Press, 2017), p. 188.

9 Rumsey, *Parish*, p. 185.

10 Gerhard Lohfink, *Does God Need the Church?* (Collegeville Minnesota: Liturgical Press, 1999), p. 262; emphasis in original.

11 Dietrich Bonhoeffer, *Life Together* (London: SCM Press, [1954] 2008), p. 17.

12 Bonhoeffer, *Life*, p. 16.

13 Bonhoeffer, *Life*, p.16.

14 Bonhoeffer, *Life*, p. 8.

15 Lohfink, *Does God Need the Church ?*, p. 262.

16 John D. Zizioulas, *The Eucharistic Communion and the World* (New York: T&T Clark, 2011), p. 128.

17 Zizioulas, *Eucharistic*, pp. 129f; emphasis in original.

Index of Names and Subjects

industrialization 24–5, 121–2

Inge, John 5, 7, 8–9, 13, 21–2

interest groups, and Fresh Expressions 72–3

internet, impact on rural life 84–5

Israel, and land 6–7

Jones, Steve 1–2

Journal of Missional Practice viii, 73–5

kingdom of God

and evangelical approach 124

and mission 79–80, 95–6, 115

land, in Old Testament 6–7

lay ministry 91, 92, 121–2, 135–6

leadership

character vs. skills 37–8

and church growth 41–2, 50, 74, 106

lay 91, 92, 121–2, 135–6

love vs. power 38–9

and personal spiritual world 39

team and gift mix 40

training for 50

and trust 38, 39

liberal approach 119–20, 122

Lightfoot, J. B. 26

Lincolnshire FEAST 95–6

listening

to community 37, 72–4, 98, 110, 112–14, 126

to God 44, 60, 96, 97–9, 129

liturgy

as drama 36

and Fresh Expressions 76

see also worship

locality

and church attendance 2–3, 32, 53–6, 122

and parish vii-viii, 18–20, 122, 132–4, 137, 140–43

re-discovery 101–116

Lohfink, Gerhard 140–41, 143

London City Mission 26